THE
BEGINNING
ENTREPRENEUR

John R. Matthews

 VGM Career Horizons
a division of *NTC Publishing Group*
Lincolnwood, Illinois USA

Library of Congress Cataloging-in-Publication Data

Matthews, John R.
   The beginning entrepreneur / John Matthews.
     p.   cm.
   ISBN 0-8442-4141-5
   1. New business enterprises—Management.   2. Entrepreneurship.
I. Title.
HD62.5.M367
658.4'21—dc20
                                                 93-1466
                                                 CIP

Published by VGM Career Horizons, a division of NTC Publishing Group
4255 West Touhy Avenue
Lincolnwood (Chicago), Illinois 60646-1975, U.S.A.
© 1994 by NTC Publishing Group. All rights reserved.
No part of this book may be reproduced, stored in a retrieval system,
or transmitted in any form or by any means,
electronic, mechanical, photocopying, recording or otherwise,
without the prior permission of NTC Publishing Group.
Manufactured in the United States of America.

3 4 5 6 7 8 9 0 VP 9 8 7 6 5 4 3 2 1

CONTENTS

INTRODUCTION

Entrepreneur is a French word meaning one who begins an enterprise and assumes the risk of failure or reaps the rewards of success. You might think entrepreneurs need to raise millions of dollars to realize their dreams. In fact, the enterprise can be humble: a student may begin a telemarketing service with nothing but a telephone and a list of leads. A successful landscape company might start as a lawn-mowing service. Many large companies started just that simply. And some of the young people now beginning simple businesses are launching the corporate giants of the future.

Who are these people we call entrepreneurs? What special qualities or abilities set them apart from others? Do inborn characteristics, like those for music or baseball, predispose someone to become an entrepreneur, or do entrepreneurs acquire their abilities through study and practice? Studies have been conducted to predict entrepreneurial success, and they suggest that education and work experience—along with strong motivational factors—help create the successful entrepreneur.

These studies found group ventures succeed better than individual efforts, and that the more highly educated the entrepreneur the better the chance of success. Successful entrepreneurs who are high school dropouts, or even college dropouts, are increasingly rare. Some dropouts do succeed spectacularly, but they could seldom be regarded as uneducated. William Gates, the billionaire founder of the Microsoft Corporation, who dropped out of Harvard, is one example of an educated entrepreneur without a degree.

Education and experience are clearly important, but what about inborn characteristics? All the studies of entrepreneurship examined nonpersonality factors, such as education, experience, and age. None yield anything close to a personality profile that could predict at an early age eventual success as an entrepreneur. Why? Perhaps because there is no such thing as a "typical" successful entrepreneur. Peter Drucker, the man who pioneered the systematic study of organizations, claims there is no entrepreneur personality profile. He says, "It [entrepreneurship] is not a personality trait; in thirty years I have seen people of the most diverse personalities and temperaments perform well in entrepreneurial challenges."

Drucker also denies that the entrepreneur is attracted to innovation and entrepreneurship because of a love of risk taking. He says, "The innovators I know are successful to the extent to which they systematically analyze the sources of innovative opportunity, then pinpoint the opportunity and exploit it. . . . Successful innovators are conservative. They have to be. They are not 'risk-focused'; they are 'opportunity-focused.' " On the other hand, some business leaders do list the willingness to take risks as a paramount entrepreneurial characteristic. An article in *New England Business* (April 1991) about whether entrepreneurship can be taught quotes Gabor Garai, a sponsor and panelist for the Enterprise Forum of the Massachusetts Institute of Technology. Garai says the major components of successful entrepreneurship are "creative spark, willingness to take risks, and ability to manage." The article further states that "A person taught to evaluate the finances of a new venture can work to narrow the risk before taking it."

The studies cite entrepreneurial traits such as being highly focused with singleness of purpose and being energetic, fearless, adventurous, and self-confident. These same qualities are often found among successful people in nonentrepreneurial fields. And, some successful entrepreneurs lack many of these "typical" entrepreneurial traits.

David McClelland, who studies and writes about achievement and motivation, analyzed test subjects' fantasies and found that people tend to be motivated by one of three things: power, achievement, or affiliation. He claims that entrepreneurs tend to fall into the second group, those motivated by achievement.

But what about people who are motivated by an obsession, or at least a fascination, with a particular product or service? Some suggest that an intense interest in the field of choice is important for success; that is probably true in many cases. Vidal Sassoon, the famous hairstylist, might not have launched his chain of salons and his line of hair care products if not for his enthusiasm for hair styling. Red Adair, whose company puts out oil-well fires, achieved success because of his passion for fire fighting. Such entrepreneurs are often described as "well-focused."

On the other hand, some entrepreneurs build large and successful companies by selecting a growing industry such as waste management. It is unlikely that they base such decisions on a lifelong love of garbage. Rather, they have, in Peter Drucker's words, "systematically analyze[d] the sources of innovative opportunity . . . and exploit[ed them]." No single approach or characteristic defines the successful entrepreneur.

Just as entrepreneurs are hard to categorize and pigeonhole, entrepreneurial ideas appear to have little systematic genesis, although planning and analysis methods can encourage nascent ideas to emerge more fully formed.

When such ideas fall on fertile ground—the prepared entrepreneur—they have a greater chance of rooting. As Edison said, "Ideas come to the prepared mind."

Many young entrepreneurs start enterprises in their early teens or younger. A story in the *Sacramento Bee* (June 3, 1991) told of several young entrepreneurs. Thirteen-year-old Kenneth Carter of Gary, Indiana, started his small catering business to earn money for expensive athletic shoes. By the time he entered college, he had catered the mayor's reelection bash and built a business worth $100,000.

Brandon Bozek of Miami created a business, Bloomin' Express, that makes weekly deliveries of fresh flowers to customers. And Jamie Bloom, a thirteen-year-old from Boca Raton, Florida, turned her hobby of decorating clothing into a business called Clever Clothes.

Perhaps the entrepreneurial success stories scattered throughout this book will inspire you, or someone you know, to launch a thriving new enterprise.

ARE YOU AN ENTREPRENEUR?

Entrepreneurs are more than just people operating small businesses. Who are they? When business people call someone an entrepreneur, the connotations are clearly complimentary. Someone who starts an especially successful business is sure to be called "a *real* entrepreneur," suggesting that whatever else entrepreneurs may be, they are always accomplished business people.

Entrepreneurs are people who develop innovative ideas and bring them to the marketplace, creating prosperity for themselves, spinoff products and services for less innovative business people, and increased economic activity for everybody. Beginning entrepreneurs sometimes spawn spinoffs if their enterprises are innovative or inspiring enough to attract the notice of other potential entrepreneurs. For example, suppose a beginning entrepreneur creates a business managing other people's garage sales. A friend may decide to manufacture T-shirts and set up a table or booth at the garage sales, paying a commission to the original entrepreneur. Success inspires both complementary businesses and competition.

Economic Activity Created by Entrepreneurs

Entrepreneurs have been around longer than free enterprise or capitalism itself. They create economic activity. Throughout history, entrepreneurs have been most responsible for

- creating new products or services,

- significantly changing existing products or services through innovation,

- creating new markets for existing products or services, or expanding the existing markets, and

- recombining or creating new uses for existing products or services.

Marketplace Innovators

The innovative entrepreneurs who first marketed personal computers spawned whole industries—software, computer peripherals such as printers and modems, and supplies such as floppy disks, printer ribbons, and tractor-fed paper. Some of these innovators began developing their projects as teenagers. Teenage entrepreneurs have been especially prominent in the computer industry. Many of them got interested because of computer games and then developed an understanding of the technology. They either had a good intuitive sense of what other users wanted or at least could foresee that millions of users like themselves would form a reliable market for computer products. They enjoyed an additional advantage because the complex technology that creates the finished personal computer incorporates many component technologies that in themselves are not complex, expensive, or difficult to produce. Thus home workshops were early suppliers to the personal computer industry. The case of Steve Jobs and Steve Wozniak of Apple Computer is well known. Less well known is the case of Michael Dell. Starting as a teenager and using only skills and resources available to any beginning entrepreneur, plus his specialized but common knowledge of personal computers, Dell launched an enterprise that became the leading manufacturer and marketer of IBM-compatible personal computers.

During his first year at the University of Texas at Austin, Dell bought and resold excess stock from dealers who could not meet the sales quota that IBM assigned to them. Once he established a reliable customer base, Dell began assembling components and selling personal computers under his own brand name. His innovative approach, which saved him considerable working capital, was to assemble the computer only after he made the sale. And because most of his sales were through mail order, the purchase price was included with orders—allowing him to leverage his cash flow into higher volume sales. Dell started the company in his dorm room in 1984. In 1993 sales are expected to reach $1.8 billion.

Who Becomes an Entrepreneur?

Do you think you might have what it takes to become a successful entrepreneur? Well, what *does* it take? As a group, successful entrepreneurs are extremely diverse, and they are scattered throughout the world, wherever entrepreneurial opportunity exists—and even in some places where it is scarce. Social scientists and psychologists have been seriously studying entrepreneurship for about twenty years, trying to find common characteristics that predict success as an entrepreneur. These characteristics mesh to form an "entrepreneurial" attitude of optimism and persistence.

The following quiz assesses some of these characteristics. Not all entrepreneurs have all these characteristics in the same degree. Some traits may be lacking altogether, but will likely be compensated for in other areas. Perhaps the one characteristic that will overcome all deficiencies is persistence.

Self-Assessment Quiz

Read each question, then select response *A* or *B,* whichever best expresses your inclinations. When you have finished, read the commentary for a brief discussion of the important entrepreneurial characteristics your choices represent.

1. You have an idea for a summer project that you believe will work. It is in a field you know little about, but you feel you

would enjoy it. A friend whose judgment you trust, and who knows something about the field, advises you that the project is beyond your abilities. How do you react?

A. You ignore the advice and rush ahead to begin the project.

B. You listen to the advice, attempt to learn more about the project by talking to others, and then proceed.

2. Graduation is approaching, and you were hoping to get into one of the top colleges. Your SAT scores are disappointing, possibly because you participated in an entrepreneurial project that seemed to sap all your free time and energy. What do you do?

A. You realistically compare your SATs to the average SATs acceptable to top schools and reluctantly decide to apply only to schools where your scores would match the average.

B. You go ahead and apply to the top schools and try to minimize your low scores by describing the impact of the entrepreneurial project on your schoolwork.

3. You join a sales group that makes cold calls on business people at their workplaces. Compensation is by commission only, and you are told to expect to make a sale about every fifth call. Following sales training, you have made twelve calls without making a sale. What is your response?

A. You know it is important to recognize unprofitable situations and cut your losses quickly, so you quit without wasting any more time.

B. You wonder if the market for the product might have changed since the training program was designed, and you begin to experiment with a different presentation.

4. You belong to a classic car club that is having its first rally in a remote rural area. Your job is to make sure there are enough food vendors at the rally so members don't have to leave the grounds to find something to eat. How do you prepare?

A. You telephone every mobile catering service in the area informing them of the rally. In addition you locate the nearest fast food outlets in case catering is not sufficient.

B. In the newspaper ad announcing the rally, you place a notice that catering services will be welcome. You also advise members that they might want to bring their own food.

5. You want to look and feel your best and decide to investigate several fitness and nutrition programs. How do you select a program?

A. A friend who lifts weights at a gym looks really good. He tells you there are numerous ways professional body builders quickly get into shape, including food supplements and some harmless drugs. You join his gym.

B. The program director at the YMCA recommends you begin a program of gentle aerobics before starting heavy-duty exercise. You join the Y.

6. You visit a business fair to find a product or service you can market. You narrow the choices to two, one of which will produce higher earnings for time spent than the other. Which product do you choose?

A. You choose a mobile car wash you can lease on a daily basis.

B. You choose a gourmet ice-cube service that markets ice made from demineralized water.

7. You are elected president of a local community service association that raises money for local charities. Each year the fund-raising goal has been increased slightly from the previous year; however, this year because of local plant closings and other negative economic trends, several experienced members of the association want to lower the goal. What do you say?

A. You disagree, arguing that the association should recruit more volunteers to maintain its history of increasing funding yearly.

    B. You propose deemphasizing the yearly increases so that in the future the organization will not depend on the town's economy to meet fund-raising goals.

8. You have a very good job but have always secretly wanted to run your own business. You have researched your venture, prepared a business plan, and found a bank willing to give you a second mortgage on your house, which you will need for capital. You estimate your venture will lose money for three years before making a profit; however, your capital should cover losses of up to five years. When your boss finds out you plan to leave, she offers you a promotion and a large salary increase. How do you respond?

    A. You accept the promotion.

    B. You continue with your venture plans.

9. You are awaiting word on whether your company will be awarded a substantial contract that you believe you have a good chance of getting. At the same time you have located a particular piece of equipment you will need to buy if you win the contract. The owner of the equipment is asking for a substantial nonrefundable down payment by a certain date, which is before you will know if you won the contract. If you don't buy the equipment (which is very hard to find), you can't fulfill the contract if you get it. If you do buy the equipment and don't get the contract, the cash drain will jeopardize the company finances. What is your decision?

    A. You buy the equipment.

    B. You don't buy the equipment.

10. You own a drug manufacturing company. Someone tampers with a bottle of your capsules and poisons several people. You locate and isolate the batch that included the poisoned capsules. You are confident that a recall of that batch will prevent further poisonings, but there is a minuscule chance that more poisoned capsules were sold and may be beyond recall. What course of action do you take?

A. You conduct a low-key recall campaign of the only batch you know to be affected, fearing that a widespread national recall would panic customers without improving safety and possibly bankrupt the company.

B. You launch a nationwide publicity campaign warning customers not to buy the capsules and offering to replace them with tamper-proof caplets.

Evaluation

The following entrepreneurial characteristics are indicated by your responses.

1. **Self-confidence.** Response *B* indicates a greater degree of self-confidence. You may lack self-confidence if you answer ''yes'' to the following questions. During a discussion of a subject you know well, do you feel insecure if someone challenges your knowledge? Do you feel insecure when someone questions your ability to perform a task you know you do well? Do you defer to the opinions of others more often than not? Do you automatically assume that others' evaluations of your abilities are more valid than your own? Do you judge your own performance more harshly than you would the performance of others? All of us have some degree of self-confidence and some degree of insecurity. What is the right balance, and how can you tell?

   Self-confidence is the characteristic that allows you to believe you can succeed in your venture. It is especially important for the entrepreneur who has experienced several previous failures, but wants to continue trying. Psychologists say self-confidence comes from having healthy self-esteem, which is the ability to feel good about and to like yourself.

2. **Optimism.** Answer *B* is the optimistic response. It is also based on the true story of a young man who wanted to attend a college where average SAT scores were well above his own. Admissions counselors told him upon his acceptance at the school that the initiative he displayed in his entrepreneurial venture offset his low SATs. Is the glass half-full or half-empty? Good luck seems to favor the optimist just as bad luck seems to pursue the pessimist.

   Entrepreneurs begin every venture expecting to succeed. Often expectations are self-fulfilling. Suppose a storekeeper is constantly pessimistic about the level of sales and therefore tends to understock inventory. Eventually some customers (those who come in after the stock runs out) will feel that they cannot find what they want in the store and will go elsewhere. A more optimistic storekeeper tries to keep a slight overstock to satisfy all customers. The pessimist may point out that the optimist will have to discount overstock at the end of the season and sell it at a loss. The optimist may counter that this loss is the worthwhile price of keeping customers happy.

Optimism, like self-confidence, is the product of healthy self-esteem.

3. **Persistence, adaptability, and the ability to deflect failure.** Response B is a good indicator of both persistence and adaptability. If you think something might be fun or interesting to accomplish, such as learning to play the piano or cook pastry, how much time will you devote to learning it before you give up and move on to something else?

Failure is a favorite subject of people who track statistics about entrepreneurship. Depending on how you read the figures, 80–95 percent of all entrepreneurial ventures fail. The figures don't say what constitutes failure or, more importantly, what happens to those who fail. The U.S. Commerce Department, which tracks new business start-ups, regards a business as a failure if it doesn't survive at least five years. What the department's figures don't account for is the number of businesses that close for reasons other than business failure. For example, some organizations are intended as short-term projects (e.g. local investment groups formed to develop a parcel of land) and are disbanded after accomplishing their goal. Some succeed so well that they are bought by larger companies and thus technically go out of business. Others may go out of business for personal reasons, such as illness, that have nothing to do with business failure. Of course, some new businesses do genuinely fail, although a much smaller percentage than 85 percent.

The figures also don't tell what becomes of the entrepreneurs who fail. Do they then get nonentrepreneurial jobs? Some undoubtedly do; however, others simply try again. Many very successful entrepreneurs have experienced failure and claim that their successes would have been impossible if not for the things they learned from their failures. Henry Ford's motor company succeeded only on the third try. Had he not been persistent, he might well have spent his career building race cars in a small shop behind his house.

4. **Preparedness and thoroughness.** Response *B* indicates both preparedness and thoroughness. How prepared and thorough are you? If you were asked to give a fifteen-minute talk before a group, would you write the speech beforehand, then read through it to time it; speak from an outline and guess when it was time to conclude; or just wing it?

   Henry Luce, founder of *Time* magazine, was famous for his thorough business conduct. Before he reprimanded an employee, made a business decision, or even sent a memo, he assembled as many facts as possible so his decisions were informed. Stanley Marcus of Neiman Marcus, long after he needed to spend time on the stores' selling floors, personally followed up any sale he made to make sure the customer was satisfied.

5. **Delayed gratification.** Response *B* is a good sign of maturity, which is often indicated by the ability to delay gratification. Very small children want their candy *now,* not after supper. Immature adults may not want to wait for the diet to kick in or the exercise program to take effect, but instead may opt for steroids for quick results. Suppose you wanted to be a doctor and had the opportunity and the ability to attend medical school. Would you decline because of the many necessary years of study before you could practice medicine?

   Many entrepreneurial ventures have similarly long time lines. Establishing a winery takes several years because vines must mature to produce grapes; another several years are necessary to perfect the wine-making process, and it takes even longer to evaluate the aging product. Even small entrepreneurial projects, such as those described in this book, require time for planning, establishing a customer base, and evaluating the venture's changes for long-term survival.

6. **Opportunity recognition.** If you guessed *B*, you are correct. A Chicago entrepreneur freezes demineralized water into 400-pound ice blocks in an oak-lined ice house, saws them into cubes, and sells them in upscale Chicago stores for almost five times the price for ordinary ice. Professor Neil Churchill,

director of Babson College's Center for Entrepreneurial Studies, said in an article in *New England Business* (April 1991) that recognizing opportunity is the most difficult aspect of entrepreneurship to teach. " 'When people say, "you can't teach entrepreneurship," that's really what they mean,' he said."

7. **Need for achievement and the ability to work hard.** Response *B* is correct. The most sought-after board members (and therefore fund-raisers) for community organizations are usually successful local entrepreneurs. Entrepreneurs are selected even in preference to nonentrepreneurs who are richer and more socially prominent citizens. Directors of nonprofit organizations confirm that the entrepreneurs are hard-working and driven to exceed previous goals. Even though their businesses are time-consuming, they still manage to devote time and hard work to their other obligations. Some writers claim entrepreneurs need high energy levels; however, it is really their need to achieve and their willingness to work hard that translates into the observed "high energy."

8. **Willingness to take, and ability to calculate, risks.** Response *B* is the correct choice for entrepreneurs, although it may not be the right choice for everyone. The entrepreneur does as much research as practical, calculates the odds for success, then makes a choice. During World War II, people who packed parachutes were required occasionally to jump wearing one of the parachutes they had packed. The entrepreneur and the parachute packer view risks in a similar manner: each works to minimize risk. To succeed as an entrepreneur, you must be willing to take risks based on your own work or your own calculations. Entrepreneurs work to minimize risks through careful research and plan to avoid failure by recruiting venture capitalists to share financial risk. This is what Peter Drucker meant when he said, "Entrepreneurs are not risk takers," but are exploiters of opportunity.

9. **Ability to handle ambiguity.** There is no correct answer to this question. Entrepreneurs often face similarly ambiguous situations in which they must make decisions and choices with incomplete information or attempt to predict future events. It would be foolhardy not to research and plan for events that

can be predicted; however, planning is not always possible. Entrepreneurs must sometimes respond to uncontrollable events and must be able to make decisions in ambiguous situations.

10. **Integrity.** Response *B* is based on a real-life situation faced by drug maker Johnson & Johnson when it discovered a bottle of Tylenol tablets had been poisoned and one person had died as a result. The company's president elected to publicize the event to alert every customer with capsules that might be poisoned. The incident cost the company approximately $150 million; however, stockholders were impressed by the company's response, massive stock sell-offs did not occur, and the company maintained its credibility by its decisive and ethical action.

Venture capitalists, when asked what quality they consider paramount in an entrepreneur, almost unanimously answer "honesty." Entrepreneurs can compensate for other characteristics they lack, but lack of integrity will ruin the most promising enterprise. Investors say no matter how attractive an investment prospect is, how good the product or service, how skilled the entrepreneur, how certain the market, if they have evidence, or even a sense, that the entrepreneur lacks integrity, they will pass up the opportunity to invest. Customers, like venture capitalists, also frequently have a sixth sense about the integrity of an enterprise, and dishonest entrepreneurs will eventually fail.

Paths to Entrepreneurship

No two people become entrepreneurs in exactly the same way. However, certain experiences do seem to encourage entrepreneurship. Most beginning entrepreneurs will identify with one or more of these typical entrepreneurial experiences.

Being Within a Supportive Framework Encouraging Individual Initiative

If your family, school, or boss encourages and rewards independent thinking and action, this will increase your chances of becoming an entrepreneur. Entrepreneurial initiative may become a natural part of your personal development. If you were lucky enough to grow up in this supportive atmosphere, you probably lack the fears and doubts that sometimes stall others. You will be more psychologically prepared to seize opportunities when they appear. As a boy, Gilman Louie was encouraged by his parents to invent his own games. He started his own computer game company when he was a sophomore in college. He later sold the business to Pergamon Press for about $1 million. This process can also work in reverse: overly controlled children may develop fears of independent action, which can limit initiative.

Being a Person with Strong Entrepreneurial Drive

If you feel you are more motivated than others by the need to achieve, have a strong ability to persevere, and are highly creative, you may strive to develop a good technical knowledge of your chosen field through education and work experience. You may desire independence or be dissatisfied working under the direction of others.

If you fall into this category and are fortunate enough to have your entrepreneurial tendencies encouraged, you are doubly blessed. On the other hand, some entrepreneurs may have been *discouraged* when showing initiative, which in turn may have precipitated rebellion and strengthened their determination and drive, much as disabled athletes are motivated to overcome handicaps.

Having Access to Financial Resources

Capital is an important aspect of entrepreneurship. Some would say it's the most important. Even enterprises generally regarded as having no overhead require *some* level of funding, if only for out-of-pocket expenses such as phone calls and photocopying. Labor—whether purchased with investment money, traded for other goods or services, or supplied by yourself and your partners can sometimes serve as a substitute for capital. However, when we refer to capital, we most often mean money.

Sometimes a small financial windfall is enough to launch an

enterprise. Many have started when, for example, a family home was sold to settle an estate, and the resulting inheritance was sufficient to completely finance a small business or else to attract additional financing from friends or venture capitalists.

Older beginning entrepreneurs may have good credit sources, or sufficient property for loan collateral, or the friendship and respect of bankers and investors. Others may be fortunate enough to have access to family money.

Being in Socially Disruptive Circumstances

Wars, famines, revolutions, and depressions displace large numbers of people into new and alien settings. Some within these groups become entrepreneurs to survive or to regain personal security or control of their lives. Many Jewish refugees now moving into Israel from the former Soviet Union are beginning small individual enterprises radically different from their former jobs. Doctors may become shopkeepers, musicians may become peddlers, teachers may take up farming. Many Oklahomans fleeing the dustbowl during the Great Depression of the 1930s became entrepreneurs in California because they couldn't find familiar work. Many Cuban refugees in Miami are also in this category, as are many Vietnamese throughout the country.

Personal tragedy and family misfortune may have similar effects. Sometimes businesses are launched through an individual's determination to completely separate from unfortunate circumstances. For example, women displaced by divorce may choose personal enterprise because no viable alternatives seem to exist.

Some choose entrepreneurship because the standard workplace doesn't accommodate their needs or abilities. Handicapped persons, particularly those confined to wheelchairs, and blind or deaf workers sometimes develop home-based businesses as an alternative to working in a corporate setting. Highly intelligent high school and college dropouts may avoid the corporate world where their lack of formal credentials presents a barrier to advancement. Two college dropouts who come to mind are Steven Wozniak, one of the founders of Apple Computer, and Michael Dell of Dell Computer. Neither could teach or hold a top engineering position in most corporations. Both were "forced" to become entrepreneurs.

Being Prepared When Opportunities Occur

Luck is the convergence of preparation and opportunity. Successful entrepreneurs actively develop opportunity through research and planning. They actively seek unmet market needs, unexploited inventions, and products and services in need of upgrading or replacement. They may even cultivate venture capital resources before finding a project.

A good illustration of this type of entrepreneur appears in a delightful anecdote from John Storey's book *Inside America's Fastest Growing Companies.* The author is describing an effort to find furnishings for his apartment in Bologna, Italy, at a local flea market:

> "*Cosa vuole?*" (What do you want?) asked one merchant. "We're looking for a rug for our apartment," we responded in laughable Italian. A large smile covered the merchant's face, and immediately feverish activity began in his stall. We were suddenly surrounded by not only the proprietor but his three brothers and two sisters. "What size, what shape, what color, what texture?" These and a dozen other questions were asked in rapid fire, staccato fashion. We tried to answer each and he said finally, "I have just the thing for you."
>
> Martha and I looked into the small sparsely stocked stall, but there was certainly nothing there that met our description. Emerging, miraculously, within minutes, were two of the younger brothers—with the exact carpet we had in mind. Of course there was nothing to say except, "How much?" We paid our 20,000 lire after a half-hearted attempt at negotiating, and went happily on our way—genuinely satisfied customers.
>
> That morning I learned something I've never forgotten: The smart Italian merchants wanted to sell us what we wanted to buy, not simply what they had in their store. In truth, the two brothers were sent running down to a competitor's stall, where they took a quick option on the piece that we were looking for, brought it back, slipped it in behind the curtain, and suddenly the merchant, to our astonishment, had what we were looking for.*

Beginning Entrepreneurship While in School

Not everyone thinks entrepreneurship is a good idea for young people still in high school, or even college. However, many studies of entrepreneurs correlate entrepreneurial success with working at

---

*Reprinted by permission of John Wiley & Sons, Inc. from John Story, *Inside America's Fastest-Growing Companies,* (New York, © 1993), pp. 49–50.

an early age and while in school. Of course, in previous generations many students worked to help support the family. Nowadays that is not as likely. Most students work to earn money for something special—a car, ski trips, expensive clothes, or stereos—and in many cases high school students work to save money for college.

Some parents and educators discourage students from working at outside jobs, especially if it's not necessary to help support the family. They point out that the student's job is to excel academically and thus prepare for further schooling or a career. Others believe that students' after-school work teaches them important social skills and work habits not learned in school.

Entrepreneurial ability is at most only partly intuitive or innate. Much of it is learned—some from books and instructors, some from doing. Unfortunately, much learning comes from making mistakes and failing. Working while in school gives you the opportunity to practice many entrepreneurial skills and learn from your mistakes and failures on a small scale. Work experience leaves you better prepared to launch your own enterprise after you have completed your education. At the same time, if you can learn from the mistakes and successes of others by reading books such as this one, so much the better.

Resources for Beginning Entrepreneurs

You will find resources on entrepreneurship close at hand. High school students have vocational education resources in the form of teachers, libraries, and shops; there are helpful organizations such as Junior Achievement, FFA, and many local work/study programs. Some high schools are now offer courses in entrepreneurial studies. For college students resources vary depending on the college. Some schools offer business courses that will accept business start-ups as course work and at the same time offer business counseling, accounting, and legal advice; marketing strategies may be devised as part of other students' course work. Some colleges are homes to "business incubators," which exist solely to aid the fledgling entrepreneur by providing such services as low-rent offices and plant space, and cooperative support services such as copying, faxing, printing, advertising, accounting, and legal services. Organizations composed of retired executives may provide, usually free of charge, advice and counseling on start-up problems.

Graduate students, especially those at prestigious research universities, may have the opportunity to participate in high-tech start-ups utilizing the technology they helped develop. Such programs may be supported by government research grants. The patents resulting from this research may be available for licensing by those who helped develop the technology. The hundreds of high-tech companies in California's Silicon Valley and along Route 128 near Boston are two examples of how university/government-supported innovation creates entrepreneurial activity that can make millionaires of those who participate, even as students.

The computer company Hewlett Packard is an example of a high-tech company started while its founders were still in graduate school. It is also a good example of a very large company that was started in home garages. Apple Computer is another example of a garage-based start-up.

Few if any of our industry giants sprang fully blown from the business planning stage to Fortune 500 status. All started many levels below the top; many, including the auto giants, started when an individual or small group decided it was time to do something different. Some acted to fulfill a dream, some to exploit an invention or innovation they believed in deeply, some simply to achieve a better living standard, and some because all other avenues seemed closed.

∇

A Case in Entrepreneurship: **HENRY FORD**

Major innovations: Introduced the concept of the automobile as a universal consumer product. Developed the modern assembly line. Demonstrated that decent wage levels expand *all* economies.

Henry Ford is rightly celebrated as the entrepreneur who put Americans on the road in cars. He was middle aged and had already experienced two business failures by the time he founded the Ford Motor Company, with the help of Alex Malcomson, in the fall of 1902. (The company began business in 1903.) Ford was already well known in the infant industry of race car building, and his winning racer, driven by Barney Oldfield, surpassed a speed of 90 miles per hour.

By the time the Ford Motor Company began operations, the French had been building cars for about a decade, and Ransom Olds, the U.S. pioneer, had been in business for several years. Ford and Malcomson began business with $100,000 capital, only about $28,000 of which was cash. Most of their assets were in the form of services or facilities. Albert Strelow, a carpenter, exchanged his wood-working shop for shares in the business, and the shop became the company's first factory. The Dodge brothers, who supplied parts for Ransom Olds, agreed to supply engines and other parts to the Ford factory, initially, in exchange for shares.

The most fortutious initial move by Malcomson and Ford was to install James Couzens as business manager. Couzens made important positive contributions to the company during its formative years, and he later became a U.S. Senator. Some historians believe it was Couzens, not Ford, who conceived the famous $5-a-day wage that thwarted attempts by the "Wobblies" (Industrial Workers of the World) to unionize the Ford plant. The wage increase gave Ford the pick of the labor market and increased productivity, which diminished the impact of

continued

the higher cost. (Approximately 30 percent of Ford workers failed to qualify for the higher wage, which also saved money.)

Nevertheless, it was Ford's genius that set the standard for the automobile industry. The Model T was more than a car model; it was a concept. Before the Model T, the automobile was beyond the financial reach of all but the richest people. Ford conceived of his car as an all-purpose tool for the farmer, who could use it for transportation, but also as an engine to saw wood, pump water, and run farm machinery. However, owners used it mostly for transportation, and sales multiplied dramatically because of the low purchase price, which in 1908 was only $850, in contrast to the $2,000 and up asked by Ford's competitors.

Lower price was not the only innovation the Model T introduced to the industry. Its global transmission, splash lubrication system, and suspension were also innovative. Its mechanical system was simple enough to allow amateur owners to repair it and keep it running, an important consideration in an era when dealers and mechanics were scarce. The Model T could negotiate rough terrain better than any of its competitors, another important advantage in an age when few towns were linked by paved highways.

Ford, like many other pioneer entrepreneurs, is often given personal credit for innovations that were actually the handiwork of employees or outside contractors. Even so, Ford had the foresight and vision to summon specialists and inventors and assure that their innovations were adopted. Although Ford is often personally credited with the assembly-line innovations that produced the Model T, it was a collaborative effort. A consultant, Walter Flanders, designed the factory that revolutionized automobile production. Flanders relied on Ford's innovations and the principles of Frederick W. Taylor, who introduced scientific management methods to the steel industry. Then Ford and his engineers tinkered with the organization, layout, and machine groupings and placements until they achieved an undreamed of level of productivity. Ford's design was revolutionary: a straight-line assembly method with each assembly tool or machine placed in the assembly line in the same sequence that parts were applied from subassemblies.

continued

This method, first used in the subassembly of parts, allowed parts on the line to flow from one work station to the next with a minimum of wasted motion. The crowning achievement of Ford's assembly method was applying this system to the assembly of the main chassis. The car was assembled, in motion, on one conveyor belt that began with a chassis frame, progressed with feeder lines of parts, and produced a finished automobile by the end of the line.

Despite his interest in innovation and the ingenious methods he devised and commissioned, Ford was suspicious of patents and inventors peddling "new gadgets and processes." Even though the Ford Motor Company bought many patents, Ford resisted paying most patent claims until forced by threat of litigation. Ford believed many patents were illegitimate, being based on old, if obscure, discoveries. In *The Last Billionaire: Henry Ford,* William C. Richards tells a story about a manufacturer who purchased a patent for an automobile shackle. Ford invited the man to visit him, telling him he had something to show him.

When the visitor arrived, Ford led him to a collection of old-time machinery piled outdoors. There, in what could have been mistaken for a junk pile, Ford pointed out a pair of ancient shackles. The shackles were the same type that the caller's recently purchased patent was presumed to cover—and the scale equipped with them was dated 1860.

"Ford patted the visitor's shoulder sympathetically. 'You thought you had something because the government granted your inventor a recent patent. I asked you here to show you the shackle was discovered by another man more than sixty years ago. It isn't really patentable.' "

Despite his many wonderful accomplishments, Ford had a darker side, which later in his life seemed to overshadow much of the good he had done for American industry. He developed a streak of anti-Semitism, which he recanted later. He contrived to fire many of the loyal and inventive employees who had provided him with the innovations that made his vast fortune possible. He attempted to withhold dividends from minority stockholders so he could force the sale of their stock at distressed prices. He engaged in paternalistic meddling into the

continued

affairs of his workers, and he arbitrarily cancelled dealership franchises if dealers failed to meet sometimes impossible quotas. Indeed, it seemed that for every innovation or act of generosity there was an equal and opposite reaction of bullheaded opposition to change or spiteful revenge against those who had served him well. Nevertheless, Ford had a vision of how the automobile should be designed, produced, priced, sold, and turned into a universal utilitarian product. And in that, he was dead right.

TYPES OF ENTREPRENEURSHIP

Analyzing different types of entrepreneurship may help you identify and choose a project. Let's examine innovative, value-added, and developmental entrepreneurship. Most beginning entrepreneurs develop projects with elements of one or more of these. Innovative entrepreneurship brings new inventions, new services, new ways of doing business, and new ways of thinking about business to the marketplace. It advances civilization and economic wealth by providing new products and services. Value-added entrepreneurship keeps the economic pot boiling. It enlarges the trading circle by giving every product and service maximum exposure to the marketplace by involving more people from the raw-material stage to the finished product or service. The third kind of entrepreneurship—developmental entrepreneurship—is what economists are thinking of when they use the term entrepreneurship. This entrepreneur develops oil fields and builds housing, skyscrapers, factories, manufacturing equipment, and other capital goods. In other words, he or she is the general partner of the capitalist. Their developments are often referred to as infrastructure, and they make up the greatest part of the "inherited wealth" of the nation that one generation passes on to another. All three types of entrepreneurship may have elements of the other two.

Innovative Entrepreneurship

Most innovative entreprenueurial ideas begin with creative solutions to everyday problems. They are small incremental improvements in the way we do business, the way we make things, or the things we make. Innovative products and services, when they first enter the market, establish a brand-new market niche and enlarge the sum total of products and services available to consumers.

Entreprenueurial innovation can be divided into global and local. Global innovations affect how business transactions are conducted or how businesses function throughout a nation, industry, or the world—or over a long period of time. Local innovation responds to special localized or one-time needs.

Global Innovation

Global innovations profoundly change the way the world works (the economy) either nationally or worldwide. When this happens you have little choice but to adapt. The personal computer industry is a major source of innovative entrepreneurship, providing innovators with opportunities to create wealth by providing products and services that never existed before. The young man, cited earlier, who invented computer games and became a millionaire is a good example of an innovative entrepreneur. Other products and services that have become major innovations include personal pagers, fax machines, obscure industrial products such as soy-based nonpolluting inks and paints, and recycling methods. These new products are called inventions. They are not innovations until entrepreneurs take them to the marketplace and make them available for general consumption.

Creating Global Innovation

Ray Kroc of McDonald's didn't invent fast food, nor did he invent franchising. He wasn't even the first to franchise fast food. Ray Kroc is credited with developing the fast food industry for the same reason Henry Ford, who did not invent the automobile, is credited with developing the automobile industry: Ray Kroc's innovations (and those of his partners) changed the rules in fundamental ways and set industry standards that all franchisors now seek to emulate in one way or another. All similar enterprises are now measured against these standards (which makes them global innovations).

Ray Kroc applied the concept of innovation in the most basic way: by taking an existing product, service, company, or industry (in his case, all of these) and changing it so significantly that henceforth all other similar operations were forced to adopt his innovations in order to compete. There was nothing new about hamburger joints. They were everywhere. Each had a gimmick: colorful awnings, flickering neon, close-up parking, car-hops, waitresses on roller skates, blaring jukeboxes. Some sold excellent hamburgers; some sold mediocre hamburgers; some were clean and attractive; others were not. Some were fast; some were slow. Some were very inexpensive, others less so. Kroc worked with all these factors and completely transformed every aspect of selling hamburgers. Every aspect of McDonald's was an innovative response to customer needs. The trademark yellow arch was designed so that customers could spot it from several miles away. The shades of yellow and orange interior and exterior decor were selected because physiological tests showed they trigger the flow of gastric juices and induce feelings of hunger. Purchasers of franchises must submit to the same sort of systematic process, both in their selection and training. Beginning with demographics, site selection is based on a comprehensive checklist, and managers and owners train and retrain on an ongoing basis. These standards now appear so uniform that many assume they were derived in some scientific way by Harvard MBAs. Instead, they were developed by many people, under the direction of Ray Kroc, who relied on trial and error, experience, intuition, and instinct in setting McDonald's policy. Now that other franchise operations have followed his lead, Kroc's methods may not seem like significant innovations, but they were. The test of their global significance is the fact that they are now fairly standard procedure in fast food—and many other franchise—businesses.

Local Innovations

Local innovations affect only one specific enterprise or, at most, enterprises in a limited area. Let's examine the case of one particularly enterprising restaurant owner who used his own innovative techniques.

Harry's Restaurant

Restaurants have an especially high rate of new-business failure.
Harry hedged some of this risk by establishing an innovative partnership with a baker.

Unlike franchises, nonfranchise restaurants must build a customer base through advertising, promotions, and word-of-mouth,
which takes money and time. In the restaurant business time is
expensive. The new McDonald's franchise owner knows before
opening how much advertising and promotion will cost and how
to handle typical start-up problems. These factors are predictable
because thousands of other franchise owners have already tested
the methods. In addition to building a customer base during the
initial opening period, the individual restaurant owner undergoes
a trial-and-error learning process that the franchise owner escapes
through hands-on supervision from the franchisor. Nonfranchised
restaurants must test new dishes, menus, prices, advertising and
promotion media, and hours of operation. They must guess how
much food to buy for each menu item because only time will tell
which dishes sell and which do not. They must establish an identity
through their choice of ethnic or American cuisine, price ranges,
levels of formality, hours of operation, credit card and check-
cashing policies. While these tests proceed, costs mount. And individual restaurant owners must cultivate numerous suppliers—
butchers and fish and vegetable vendors—whereas the McDonald's
owner simply offloads all supplies from a McDonald's supply truck
that stops on a scheduled basis. No wonder franchising is so popular. It is not, however, entreprenuerial and innovative. Ray Kroc
has already supplied all the innovation that McDonald's can toler-
ate, and any franchisees who introduced further innovation by
departing from established standards would violate their contract
and lose their franchise license.

Harry's restaurant and the bakery, his co-tenant, greatly reduced their financial risk by adapting some global innovations pioneered by franchisors—without purchasing a franchise. They
then added some local innovations of their own. Harry's reasons
for not buying a franchise are the same reasons most franchisees
choose *to* buy. The investment capital required is about the same,
but future profitability—offset by greater risk—is potentially
greater for the nonfranchise restaurant. Harry hired a McDonald's
manager as a consultant before designing and locating his restaurant. The consultant provided franchise expertise on the following

factors: finding and interpreting demographic data to forecast size of customer base, building locations, and pricing policies; layout and design of kitchen and service facilities; decor and furnishing strategies appropriate to price range and ambience goals; and guidelines for personnel policies and employee training. The restaurant is fairly expensive and full-service—unlike McDonald's—so both Harry and the consultant had to extrapolate their data to fit different circumstances. If Harry had just wanted to copy McDonald's, he would have bought a franchise instead of hiring a consultant. He didn't need the consultant to teach him about cuisine; he was an experienced chef with strong ideas and previous success. Harry was interested in those universal aspects of McDonald's success: how to get, please, and retain customers.

Harry's local innovation was sharing many of his capital goods and his site with his co-tenant, a bakery that markets high-quality French and Italian pastries to expensive restaurants. Harry and the baker, Susan, are both experienced in their fields. Harry managed a restaurant very similar to his own. As manager of the first restaurant, Harry was responsible for all phases of the operation—from hiring personnel to setting promotion policy and doing the bookkeeping. Susan, who has a sales background, worked as a baker during her entire college career and recently completed a pastry course at the Culinary Institute in New York state. Both obtained financial backing for their enterprises and their backers are confident of their chances for success. Still, they face that very high rate of restaurant failure.

Tom and Susan consider themselves ideal partners in many ways, and they regard sharing a facility as a good way for each to save about one-third on their initial investment. Both the restaurant and the bakery need many of the same appliances and tools. They can also share computerized bookkeeping and record-keeping equipment. Both operate at different times. The restaurant kitchen closes at nine, and cleanup is completed before the bakery opens at eleven.

In addition to their equipment and facility, the two businesses also share some personnel and services: the computer operator maintains records for both, and the cost of the cleaning crew, utilities, and telephones is prorated. In addition each business provides the other with needed support and advice. The restaurant is a customer of the bakery, and the bakery put a retail counter in the front of the restaurant, which attracts traffic for both businesses.

In an informal evaluation at the end of the first operating year, both owners agreed that the mutually supporting enterprises probably saved one or both from going out of business during the first year. The shared facility was an especially important advantage for the restaurant, which seemed adequately financed, but took longer than expected to develop a customer base. As Harry remarked, "It doesn't take a large miscalculation about customer turnover to sink a new restaurant. Suppose you expect to average 40 diners per day in the first month of operation, and you get only 35. That doesn't seem like a large numerical miscalculation, but translated into dollars it's about $100 per day, which is more than I budgeted to live on during the start-up period. And, unfortunately, expenses don't drop proportionately; in a restaurant, they don't drop at all. You still need all your waiters and kitchen personnel; utilities don't drop, and you don't even save much on food supplies because you don't know which days sales will be down. If we didn't have the bakery to help absorb expenses, I'm convinced the restaurant would not have survived the simple miscalculation."

Some local innovations may simply be unique ways to solve a specific problem. Nineteen-year-old Braun Mincher saw a business opportunity when Colorado legalized casino gambling in several mountain towns. Cripple Creek, a tiny town of 600 reached only by narrow mountain roads, lacked sufficient parking space for potential casino customers. Mincher developed a business plan and enlisted a financial partner to solve the parking problem. The result is Western Star Charters, which transports customers from Denver to the new casinos. According to an article in *Nation's Business* (December 1992), Mincher convinced casino operators to provide his customers with enticements such as free drinks and buffet luncheons.

"'So everybody is happy,' says Mincher. 'The casino get the people at their place, we get the business, and the customer doesn't have to worry about driving.'"

Like Mincher, you may become an innovative entrepreneur by discovering something unique that others are willing to buy. Here are some other examples. Students at the University of Southern California produce their newsletter on audiocassettes, thus eliminating printed copy, and disseminating their newsletter more efficiently and cheaply. Production and mailing costs were reduced from two to three dollars for the traditional newsletter to about a dollar for the audiocassette. The newsletter tapes are mailed to alumni, colleagues at other colleges, and others interested in the students' program. If publishers of other newsletters adopt the practice, the students' audio newsletter could become an important global innovation. Another innovative beginning entrepreneur hauls away lawn clippings, leaves, limbs, and other plant matter free of charge; he then sells them to a local landscape service that makes it own compost. The young entrepreneur's service—free debris removal—did not exist previously, and thus is innovative.

Value-Added Entrepreneurship

The concept of value-added entrepreneurship applies to both products and services and may also be an important element in other types of entrepreneurship. Building houses adds value to land. Braun Mincher's innovative transport service, mentioned earlier, adds value to the casino gambling industry, and thus income to the geographic region. That is why the casino operators were willing to provide free meals and drinks to Mincher's clients.

Bread is a good example of a value-added product. Farmers produce wheat. The miller adds value to the wheat by processing it into flour; the baker adds value by making it into bread; the supermarket adds value by making it convenient for the consumer to buy. Farmers in Texas are rediscovering value-added economics (which they learned about many years ago when cotton gins added value to their cotton crops). The agriculture commissioner is promoting investment in fabric mills and other processing facilities so the region can export value-added products rather than raw materials. He is choosing this strategy because the cost of adding value is much less than the market value of the resulting products. Thus, the entire regional economy is boosted through value-added economics.

Beginning entrepreneurs can, and do, find similar rewards in value-added products and services. T-shirts are one example. Those with commercial logos are very popular—and considerably more costly than plain white T-shirts. The value-added chain of the T-shirt starts in the field. The farmer sells cotton to the ginner, who add value by processing it into clean fiber that can be sold to the fabric mill. The mill adds value by weaving it into cloth, which is sold to garment makers who add value by manufacturing T-shirts. At this point the beginning entrepreneur enters the picture, purchases the T-shirts, silk screens designs onto them—which add considerable value for the person who wears them—then sells the final value-added product at flea markets, garage sales, school fairs, and perhaps through mail order.

A young entrepreneur of fifteen, Susan E. Behm of Westminster, Colorado, won a 1992 "Woman of Enterprise" award from Avon Products and the U.S. Small Business Administration for her value-added entreprenueurial project. Using computerized embroidery equipment provided by her mother, a consultant to the embroidery industry, Susan founded a company called Susie Q's Embroidery, which embroiders sweatshirts, T-shirts, bags, jackets, and towels.

Perhaps the most familiar example of value-added entrepreneurship is retail stores. It would be extremely inconvenient for consumers to visit manufacturers to buy the merchandise found in most retail stores. Clothing stores are a good example. Few people live near a clothing manufacturer, and even if they did, that manufacturer would probably provide only a limited range of selections (although in vast quantities). The local manufacturer might specialize in one type of clothing, such as blue jeans or children's clothes. A consumer would have to visit many factories all across the country (and overseas) to find the selection available in even the smallest retail clothing store. The retailer, then, provides many value-added services to the consumer, not the least of which is variety of selections. Of course, consumers pay for this value-added service. The cost added at every step of the value-added process provides the entrepreneur's profit. However, most consumers, faced with the alternative of finding the goods they need from the manufacturing source, would agree that the additional cost is fully justified. Consumers would probably pay more for these services in the long run if they had to go to manufacturers than they currently do for retail products. Other value-added services the clothing retailer provides, in addition to variety of selection, include the following:

- **Location.** The smart retailer chooses an easy-to-find area, convenient for customers, with ample parking, usually near other retailers.

- **Merchandise selection**. Retailers keep abreast of fashion so customers are assured their selections follow current clothing trends.

- **Alterations**. The retailer makes sure garments fit properly before the customer takes them home.

- **Satisfaction guarantees**. Almost every retailer accepts returned merchandise if the customer is unhappy with it.

- **Financing**. Many retailers offer private charge plans, or at the least accept bank credit cards.

- **Delivery**. Most upscale clothing retailers will deliver merchandise to customers' homes.

A young woman, Cindy, needed extra money for college, and wanted to work with children. She devised an innovative and value-added child-care project. In the next chapter, we will examine how Cindy selected her project through research, decided on its form, and worked through some of the start-up problems.

A Case in Entrepreneurship: **MARY KAY ASH**

Major innovation: Introduced seminar selling to direct sales in cosmetics.

Mary Kay Ash first went to work after her husband left her with three children to support. The job she took as a sales representative for the Stanley Home Products Company, which sold cleaning products through demonstrations in the home, helped her develop her later entreprenueurial venture, Mary Kay Cosmetics. At Stanley she learned about selling, and she learned self-confidence. By 1963 she thought she was ready to retire and write a how-to book for women who wanted to enter sales; then she thought, why not begin a company that would employ women sales representatives rather than just write about it? That is what she did.

Mary Kay began her business in downtown Dallas in a 500-

continued

square-foot storefront and called it Beauty by Mary Kay. It featured unique skin-care products that she bought from another entrepreneur, who developed the products with the help of her father, a hide tanner. The tanner noticed that his hands looked much younger than his face, and he suspected that the solution he used for tanning hides was responsible, so he began using it on his face. His daughter quickly recognized the potential for a women's skin care product; together they developed a face cream, eventually selling the rights to Mary Kay.

When Mary Kay Ash began her direct-sales Mary Kay Cosmetics business she went up against the giant of the industry; the only other cosmetic company to use direct sales was Avon. Her sales method—teaching skin care in the home rather than straight door-to-door sales—was innovative for the cosmetics industry, but not entirely new; she adapted it from the Stanley Home Products method.

Mary Kay trained her representatives to conduct skin-care seminars (skin care was Avon's weakest area). She emphasized the superior quality of her cosmetics to maintain and promote good skin health. Joseph and Suzy Fucini in *Entrepreneurs: The Men and Women Behind Famous Brand Names and How They Made It*, describe Mary Kay's innovative sales method:

> Instead of simply going door to door to drop off catalogs and take orders, Mary Kay's salespeople conducted two-hour "beauty shows" in the homes of women who agreed to act as hostesses. Participants at each show were treated to a talk on skin care and a personalized makeup lesson. The beauty shows required greater effort on the part of the sales force, but they helped interest more women in trying the firm's skin care products.

Sales representatives are also recruited at the beauty shows. Each new representative buys a Beauty Kit, which must be paid for with a money order or cashier's check. Mary Kay, having seen other direct-sales companies go broke from loose credit practices, has very stringent credit policies and does not allow any representative, not even the most successful or the longest employed, to buy on credit. Representatives must also pay for their own transportation, meals, and lodging when attending training seminars and company conventions. Mary Kay treats her representatives like independent business associates, which is what they are.

continued

In addition to her unique sales method, Mary Kay employs some unusual incentives to keep her sales force motivated. She conducts frequent sales meetings for her representatives at which she awards prizes for achievement; she provides ample opportunity for top producers to advance up the managerial ladder through regional and territorial positions of sales director, a method now widely copied by other direct sales organizations. Her most unusual method is allowing her top producers the use of a pink Cadillac. (Lesser performers may be given the use of a pink Buick.) Mary Kay representatives *can* make it big; *Working Woman* magazine (May 1989) reported that Shirley Hutton, after selling for Mary Kay for sixteen years, had a net worth of $3 million dollars and was making $400,000 per year.

CHOOSING YOUR BUSINESS OR PRODUCT

To choose the right business or project, you must first find what the marketplace will accept that you are capable of providing. Then, select the project you would enjoy sufficiently to overcome all obstacles to success.

The Marketplace

Richard M. White, Jr., in his excellent book *The Entrepreneur's Manual,* describes a method for identifying viable entrepreneurial projects that he calls *market gap analysis.* To apply White's method, an entrepreneur identifies broad objectives, then segments elements of the particular industry in numerous ways to identify unmet needs (market opportunities). Further segmentation then begins to produce ideas for products and services that meet those needs. White's method assumes a mature entrepreneur knowledgeable about a particular market or industry. You don't need anything as sophisticated as White's methodology; however, some elements of gap analysis have been adapted here for use by beginning entrepreneurs.

Product or Service

You may know well in advance of beginning your enterprise just what product or service you want to offer. For some, circumstances suggest or dictate the product or service. If you live near a well-populated beach and want a summers-only project, a service or product that would sell to beach-goers is a natural choice.

Using a variation of White's market gap analysis, you can develop criteria to focus your choices. For this exercise on choosing a project, take several blank sheets of paper and label them as follows:

- Needs List
- Areas of Interest
  Activities
  Subjects
  Objects
  Abstractions and Unclassifiable Likes
  Hobbies
  Pastimes
  People

- Areas of Ability

- Assets

- Areas of Opportunity

- Restrictions and Limitations
  Geographic
  Financial
  Skill and Education
  Size
  Time

Here are some examples from the combined lists of several college students searching for a joint enterprise.

Needs List

Money for car
Money for school
A way to support an expensive hobby

Areas of Interest

Activities List

Golf
Woodworking
Cooking
Softball
Flying
Singing
Playing the piano

Subjects List

Math
Medicine
Education
Religion
Food
Sports
Music

Objects List

Cars
Trains
Planes
Computers
Furniture

Abstractions and Unclassifiable Likes List

Cool spring mornings
Freedom
Self-discipline

continued

Cooperation
Independent thinking

Hobbies List

Stamp collecting
Bird watching
Sewing
Computer club

Pastimes List

Reading
Watching TV
Chess

People List

Teachers
Coaches
Scientists
Astronauts

Areas of Ability and Assets

Abilities:

Math
Teaching children
Following instructions
Calligraphy
Driving

Assets:

A computer
A car
Sports equipment
Sewing machine

Areas of Opportunity

You may have already thought of several opportunities for businesses. Write them down. Don't be concerned now with whether they are practical or do-able. If they are not, they may still suggest other and better options. Another hint: What do you hear people complaining about? Petty complaints such as "the shopping mall is too far away" or "my house plants look awful" may inspire ideas for money-making projects. Don't worry about whether the concerns you identify suggest projects. Later, you can discard those that do not. Your list may look like this:

Taxes

Lack of free time

Housework/Lack of household help

Lack of quality time with family

Bureaucracy

Neglected houseplants

Children get out of school at different times and at different schools

Restrictions and Limitations

Your choices will narrow as you identify restrictions that limit your potential project list. Some restrictions are self-imposed; for example, you may not wish to work at night or travel out of town. Other restrictions are dictated by circumstances, such as geography. (If you live in the central United States, you probably won't sell surfboards.) You might also face financial or educational restrictions. As a beginning entrepreneur, you probably have limited start-up funds and not enough specialized training or resources to compete with contractors, manufacturers, or developers; however, you may have opportunities to supply goods to larger enterprises. The college students in this example segmented their Restrictions and Limitations List as follows:

Geographic

Does not require relocation. (Most beginning entrepreneurs need to rely on their current support system.)

Financial

Does not require investment. (Most beginning entrepreneurs don't have investment capital and can't raise any, at least not during the initial stages of their projects.)
Cash-only sales. (Eliminating accounts receivable reduces the need for working capital.)

Skill and Education

Can be performed by unskilled workers or falls within the scope of the entrepreneur's own skills.

Size

Is suitable for several partners. (Most entrepreneurs can't afford to hire employees during the initial stages of their enterprise, so workers must buy into the business with their labor.)

Time

No time restrictions

As you add criteria, the restrictions begin to narrow the scope of possible projects. At this point you may begin to consider projects such as garden maintenance and lawn mowing, errand running, and chauffeuring the elderly. Some young entrepreneurs, like Cindy in the next example, have special abilities and interests, and some notion of the general field they want to enter, but no clear idea how to get started. Cindy did some simple segmenting exercises that began to narrow her interests and suggest concrete projects. The nature of her service actually evolved during the planning process; it was a somewhat different, but vastly improved, version of her original idea. Other entrepreneurs simply try to determine the following criteria: what is available, what do they know about, what can they fund, and what interests them.

Combining Your Lists

The next step is to take your lists and spread them out side by side. With a highlighting pen, mark those entries that you feel more strongly about. Do not discard the leftovers; they may become useful later on. On a separate sheet of paper, list the highlighted items side by side in columns. If you have partners or potential partners, combine your lists. This is a good time for a brainstorming session, a free-association business meeting. It's hard to describe or dictate a precise method for this process, but as you begin looking at your lists side by side, ideas for viable projects will emerge. When one does, write it down on a separate sheet of paper, with perhaps a sentence or paragraph explaining it.

Here's an example of how this might work. The example lists given earlier are the highlighted items from much longer lists created by two young partners, first-year women college students. By lining up their likes, skills, opportunities, assets, and restrictions side by side and discussing them, they identified five or six viable, interesting, and workable projects. They finally chose a project based on the following clues from their combined lists:

Likes	Skills	Opportunities	Assets	Restrictions
computers	organizing	taxes	computer	all listed
		household help		

Using these clues as a basis for brainstorming, the combination of taxes and difficulty with household help triggered a discussion of Zoe Baird, who lost the nomination for Attorney General of the United States because she failed to comply with the law requiring her to withhold payroll taxes for her live-in nanny. One partner recalled reading in a news story that people who employ even casual baby-sitting help and pay out more than $50 in a quarter must withhold and report taxes. The other partner recalled reading (in a newsletter from the publisher of her computer accounting software) that four high school girls started a baby-sitting consortium, using the computer to track their fees. "Why not," the second partner said, "do something similar, except in addition to keeping track of wages, we could also handle all tax filings. It would work like a temporary employment agency. The parents would contract with us, and we would supply the baby-sitters." Because of the publicity generated by the Zoe Baird case, the young women were able to develop a client list using fliers, word of mouth, and a telemarketing sales strategy. They now plan to expand their service to include individuals who clean houses, mow lawns, run errands, and perform other household chores for pay.

Another college student, a young man, used the method above to develop a home recycling service. The clues he used from his lists were the following:

Likes	Skills	Opportunities	Assets	Restrictions
clean air	selling	people begin recycling projects then abandon them	truck	no money

Going door to door, he began to provide families with recycling supplies—containers for separating out glass, aluminum, plastics, and newspapers. He delivers supplies free of charge, exchanges them for recyclable refuse, then sells the refuse at the local recycling center. He also offers his clients free garage and attic clean-outs in exchange for items he can sell at flea markets. In addition to using the above exercise, he was also partly inspired by a news report on TV about a formerly homeless man in New York City who buys aluminum cans from homeless people for a penny each and sells them for a nickel at the recycling center.

Note that all these entrepreneurs were well informed about current events. If the young women had not been aware of the Zoe Baird affair and the law requiring withholding of taxes for even casual babysitters, they probably would not have uncovered their business opportunity.

Once you identify one or several viable projects, perform one last useful check—search for fatal flaws. A fatal flaw is an obstacle you can't readily or practically overcome and that could prevent you from realizing your project. Most fatal flaws can be eliminated with your restrictions and limitations checklist; however, you should double check. Here are some useful questions for uncovering fatal flaws:

Does it [your project idea] violate any laws or ordinances such as zoning, sign, or parking restrictions?

Does it violate any physical or mathematical laws (e.g., would the product cost more to make than you could sell it for)?

Does it require any licenses or permits you can't readily obtain?

Does it require any skills or abilities you don't have and can't readily learn?

Cindy's Child-Care Project

Cindy, a college student, used her own variation of market gap analysis to identify and plan a business that grew into a career and profitable lifetime enterprise. You may find her background and situation similar to your own. Let's examine her enterprise in some detail.

Background

Cindy is a twenty-year-old college student living at home with her parents. She is an average student who works hard at her studies, and she vaguely defines her career goal as "wanting to work with children." Although her specific goals are unformed, she feels strongly about children and will eventually seek teacher certification. As a teenager she worked as a baby-sitter. She is well organized and methodical.

At the end of her second year of college, she finds she has depleted much of the money she and her parents saved for her education. She is ineligible for scholarship aid. Although she does qualify for student loans, she wants to keep her debt to a minimum. Her parents have agreed to match whatever money she earns.

Even though her long-range goals are still vague, Cindy's medium-range and short-term goals are clear: she must finish two more years of college. Obviously, she must begin to earn some money, but she also needs ample time and energy for her schoolwork. Her monthly expenses, including tuition and other prorated school expenses, come to about $2,000.

Faced with the need to earn money for school, Cindy first makes a "needs list," even before she knows she will become an entrepreneur.

Cindy's Needs List

1. $200–$300 per week

2. Evening or weekend work only

3. Sufficient free time for study

4. Flexible work schedule to allow for extra study at exam time

At the bottom of the list Cindy writes "child-related." This is not an absolute need, but it is a goal. Cindy wants to find work that will also provide her some personal satisfaction.

Cindy's only work experience is baby-sitting while in high school. She likes children and wants to continue baby-sitting while in college, but baby-sitting doesn't meet all Cindy's needs based on her checklist. It meets needs 2, 3, and 4 beautifully.

2. Baby-sitting jobs are almost always at night or on the weekends.

3. Baby-sitting is one of the few jobs that allows for plenty of time on the job for study, especially after the children are in bed.

4. By refusing sitting assignments at exam time, she can have the flexibility to attend tutoring sessions or visit the library.

Despite all these advantages, baby-sitting would never meet Cindy's first need, which is to earn $200 to $300 per week.

She looks at other job prospects. Clerking at a convenience store—if she worked full-time—would provide the income she needs. Convenience stores are open at night, so the night shift would provide the right hours. However, she would have no time to study and no schedule flexibility, so she keeps searching.

Next, she considers applying to work as a night clerk in a motel; that would satisfy her first three needs, but wouldn't give her any flexibility at exam time. Cindy even briefly considers taking a full-time day job and going to school part-time. Clearly she needs a much more radical solution to her employment problem than she would ever find as a low-skilled wage earner. Cindy feels it's a shame that baby-sitting is such an unattractive prospect for earning money.

Using White's gap analysis, Cindy decides to systematically analyze her situation. She already knows that child-care is the market area she wants to investigate. The gap analysis process seems simple and begins by segmenting the target market and restricting the choices to viable options. There are many ways to do this. One good way is to break into simple components the product, service, market, competition, and any other component relating to the market. Cindy sees the process is somewhat like diagramming a sentence to find the subject and predicate.

One way to segment is horizontally, which would mean taking a broad look at the child-care and child-activity industry, perhaps looking at manufacturers who supply schools and parents with educational toys and other goods to amuse children. Another way to segment would be vertically, by breaking down a typical child's day into separate functions. Cindy senses that vertical segmentation is the better choice in her case.

She first looks at the various kinds of child-care to see if she can generate a "bright idea." She lists the components of a child's day and beside them puts the agencies or factors affecting the child. When she finishes, Cindy's list looks like this:

1. Early morning; breakfast—parents

2. Midmorning to midafternoon; school or free time, depending on the age of the child—teachers, parents, or child-care agency

3. Late afternoon to early evening; after-school program or home—after-school agency such as YMCA, Boys Club, church; or parents

4. Evening; supper—parents or baby-sitter

Cindy then examined this list one segment at a time in her search for a "bright idea." Here are notes and thoughts as she analyzed each part of the child's day:

1. *Early morning; breakfast—parents.* The only possibility for paid work at this stage is for a live-in nanny or "au pair" girl. Probably not worth pursuing.

2. *Midmorning to midafternoon; school or day-care.* Competing for day-care clients is out of the question. I am at school in the daytime. Besides, setting up a day-care center requires licensing and investment, along with some very rigid scheduling that

would interfere with school even if I switched all my classes to the evening. What about care services for school-age kids? What enterprise would involve direct contact with these kids other than starting a private school? I'm still studying to be a teacher, so I'm not yet qualified to start a school. On the other hand, when I was in sixth grade, I had a math tutor who was a college student. I'll jot down the word *tutor* and maybe come back to it later. Advantage: if I tutor, I can easily tutor three or four kids at a time.

3. *Late afternoon to early evening—after-school program or home.* What kind of after-school program could I offer that could compete with basketball at the Y or the many free after-school programs public schools are beginning to offer? Advantage: If I can think of something to offer, I can probably assemble a small group, which would obviously pay more and probably be more fun for the kids to boot. Which kids are not served by existing programs? This might require further segmentation. Put a check mark by this one and come back to it later.

4. *Evening; supper—parents or baby-sitter.* Here we are, full circle, back to baby-sitting. As much as I would enjoy it, I need to earn more money for college than I did during high school, when I worked for next to nothing. Something keeps dragging me back to baby-sitting. I'll look at my needs list to see if I can figure it out. Oh, I see—it's evenings and flexible scheduling that make it so attractive. Maybe if I review this list of options, I will find some way to combine their advantages with the flexible schedule I need.

Cindy immediately sees that the attraction of day-care, tutoring, and after-school programs is the possibility of building small groups of client kids, thus earning an attractive compensation rate. She also immediately sees problems. While she could easily baby-sit a group of five to ten kids, to do so she must convince parents to bring the children to her rather than going into the children's homes. When parents return from a late evening out, they don't like to awaken their children to take them home. At the same time, they may be reluctant to let the children spend the night at the baby-sitter's. While it's not unheard of for parents to drop off children at the baby-sitter's, it's much more usual for the baby-sitter to come to the child's home. Besides, they will resent paying regular baby-sitter fees to what they see as an assembly-line operation.

There is also a logistical problem. Assuming she can overcome the other obstacles, can she physically handle ten kids staying overnight? Her parents give her the use of the basement playroom, the guest bedroom, and, of course, her own room for her project. Suppose she lived in a dormitory 500 miles from her parents' home. Without the advantage of using her parents' home, Cindy would simply have gone back to item four and continued the segmentation process until she found a viable option.

Note that for this process to work well you must recognize impenetrable roadblocks when they occur so you can move on in other directions. If Cindy finished her education and determined that this evening child-care project was her final career goal, she could certainly overcome this logistical obstacle. However, she needs a project that fits her current goals and is in keeping with her school schedule. Therefore she is sensible enough not to become enmeshed in a project that would interfere with her long-range goals.

After about an hour of making lists, drawing arrows, and scratching out notes, Cindy has something that seems to fit her requirements. It is child-related, and its schedule can be flexible; she can schedule for Friday and Saturday nights and can shut down completely just before finals without losing her client base. It doesn't require capital or a long lead time for her to begin working and earning money, and by charging parents only what they would pay an in-home baby-sitter, Cindy can still earn as much working two nights per week as she could working full-time at a fast food restaurant.

And so the concept for Kids' Overnight Adventure is born. However, Cindy is still not ready to begin her project. She still has some preliminary work to do. She still needs to research her market, prepare a business plan with a budget, and test her idea. We will follow her progress in the following chapters.

A Case in Entrepreneurship: **JOHN SHEPHERD**

Major innovation: Developed unique system of work place promotion, which encourages placing janitorial subcontractor's employees in industrial jobs.

John Shepherd is the son of a working-class black family that migrated to Chicago in 1938 when he was five years old. Like many entrepreneurs, he began working independently early. At age nine he built shoeshine kits and franchised them to other boys for a fee. Shepherd's first adult effort at becoming an independent business owner ended in failure, as do most first efforts. He bought a small grocery in the Chicago neighborhood where he lived, where he had worked as a stock boy, delivery boy, and butcher. He went out of business after a chain supermarket opened nearby and his customer base deserted him—except for those who needed to buy on credit, a service the chain didn't provide. Philip Drotning and Wesley South, in *Up from the Ghetto,* quote Shepherd on that early experience:

"It wasn't long before I discovered that all of my customers were credit customers and all the cash customers were going to the A&P. . . . I was selling a lot of groceries, but it was all on the books. I finally had to fold, and I resolved then and there that I would be an independent businessman again, but not where I had to carry everything on credit in a 'Mom and Pop' type of store."

Shepherd later formed a janitorial contracting service called the Dale Maintenance Company, after experimenting with a heavy-duty household cleaning service that generated lots of business but made little money. He decided the Dale Company would concentrate only on industrial contract jobs.

One of Shepherd's principal business tenets was establishing a thorough job-training program. Most of his recruits, both blacks and whites, are from the Chicago ghettos, many with

continued

troubled backgrounds, some from neighborhood gangs, others with prison records or on public welfare roles. He teaches good work habits, cleanliness, and the necessary skills for maintenance work. He pays above the prevailing wage and promotes strictly on a merit basis.

The opportunity to work at Shepherd's company is more than just a chance at a lifetime occupation in maintenance work. In a unique agreement with client firms, his employees have the opportunity to be promoted from his firm to industrial jobs with the client firms. In this way he supplies entry-level employees and work place training for his clients. Drotning and South explain:

> An employee of Shepherd's, working in the maintenance crew at Universal Oil Products Company, is interviewed for employment with that company after he has been working in the plant for a year. If he is found to be qualified for a more responsible position with that firm, Shepherd cheerfully releases him to UOP.
>
> Many of his employees have established themselves in lifetime careers through this process. The first to make it was a lady who had been on Aid to Dependent Children, who began working for Shepherd cleaning floors, advanced to shift supervisor, and then went to work for the firm whose floors she had been scrubbing as receptionist at the front desk in their general office building.

Shepherd has also developed an industrial security operation and a drywall construction company that subcontracts for general contractors. He preaches self-sufficiency to his employees and the concept they will rise by their own efforts. To demonstrate his commitment to the concept, he refuses government funding for his unique training and placement program, even though some would qualify for government grants that reimburse job-training costs. Like most entrepreneurs, he is committed to making his own way through his own efforts.

4

RESEARCHING YOUR MARKET

Near the intersection of two busy streets is an older but attractive building, usually uninhabited, that has housed a series of fast food restaurants for very brief periods. During the last five years, at least three restaurants have opened at the site, then quickly closed. Next door is a franchised fast food restaurant. A large medical center is two blocks away; another two or three blocks beyond that is a small university. Conventional wisdom has led several restaurant entrepreneurs to believe it's an ideal place for a fast food business because it's near a busy intersection with another fast food outlet that draws lots of traffic, and it has a large potential customer base nearby. For whatever reason, conventional wisdom was wrong. One thing is certain: simple research would have revealed that previous efforts to establish restaurants at that site failed. Each entrepreneur whose business failed on the site either ignored this important information or never bothered to acquire it. Common sense research could have saved those entrepreneurs a great deal of work, effort, and money.

You may have already started your market research. The process of identifying viable businesses, described in Chapter 3, involves answering two basic market research questions: Is there a need (market) for your identified product or service or can one be created? And can you gain access to the market with the resources of your company? If you did your segmenting exercises properly in the last chapter, the answer to both questions is "yes." However, that is hardly enough.

Marketing

Marketing is am umbrella term encompassing many different functions, including advertising, sales, sales promotion, package design, direct mail selling, and some aspects of public relations. Research is the process of gathering information to answer questions already formulated, so it is crucial before beginning to have enough information to formulate the right questions. The easiest way to begin is to list relevant and *known* data you already have, being careful not to make any unwarranted assumptions. This last point—as the failed fast food entrepreneurs discovered—is key. Wrong or skewed data can completely derail a marketing effort. A well-known example of a marketing strategy based on inaccurate assumptions involves the generally successful Campbell Soup Company. In the early part of this century, the *Saturday Evening Post* attempted to persuade Campbell to advertise in its pages, only to be told that the *Post* was the wrong medium for Campbell's Soup because *Post* readers were working class people, while Campbell's customers were upper income. The *Post*'s advertising sales representatives suspected that Campbell's was wrong about its customer profile, and to prove it they put their own market research department to work. The director of the project rented a National Guard armory and arranged to have garbage picked up in several Philadelphia neighborhoods, both working class and upper income. The collected garbage was brought to the armory and sifted for Campbell's Soup cans. As the *Post*'s advertising sales staff suspected, more cans were found in working class garbage than in upper income. As a result Campbell's was able to better target its advertising budget (and became an advertiser in the *Saturday Evening Post*).

Market Research

Careful market research includes the following standard types of information.

Types of Information You Need

1. Customer profile: Who will use your product or service? If you have a baby-sitting service, your customers will be restricted to those who have children too young to leave home alone.

2. Potential market size (numerical): Out of the total population of your marketing area, how many people would need your product or service?

3. Geographic boundaries of market area: Common sense and experience will usually suffice to determine how far you can generally go to serve your customers.

4. Competition: A thorough assessment of your competitors' performance will tell you how hard you must work to compete.

5. Pricing: The easiest way to set pricing is to survey your competitors' pricing; if it is uniform, perhaps you should conform, but if it varies you may want to differentiate your service using a lower price/higher efficiency, higher price/higher quality, or additional service strategy.

6. Any special information that would apply to your own particular case.

Where Will You Get the Information?

Beginning entrepreneurs can use several simple procedures to make market assessments. Many are just simple common sense.

1. Read newspapers and trade magazines to become knowledgeable about industry-specific trends and projections of future changes in markets.

2. Get a classified phone book and count the number of competitive businesses. Call them up, posing as a possible customer, to assess price information, product availability, services offered, delivery response time, and general competence.

3. Conduct physical surveys. Drive around town and look closely at competition. Do they appear prosperous? Are they

well located? Are they clustered in one area? If possible speak with customers to measure their level of satisfaction. And most important: Do the businesses appear to have too much or too little business?

4. Talk to bankers whose clients own businesses similar to yours. Bankers who make loans to businesses know better than anyone else in the community the general market health of any given product or service, whether it is overrepresented or underrepresented, and the state of the competition.

5. Analyze newspaper and television advertising. Who is advertising? What is the quality of the ads? Do they project a sense of success or desperation? Why?

6. Use the library. It's the ultimate research tool for finding demographic information, industry-specific magazines, and skilled researchers ready to help.

7. Survey the market by devising your own questionnaire. However, beware of questionnaire-based market research. Remember, the Edsel was developed from information gathered in broad-based market surveys.

8. If you live near a college or university, call the business department and find out if business students are available to design and conduct market research.

9. Consult marketing books for both general ideas and specific strategies.

10. Visit a business incubator for general guidance or referral to SCORE (Service Core of Retired Executives) volunteers with marketing experience.

11. Interview people with experience in your field or cultivate mentors who can advise and counsel you.

Common Sense Market Research

Common sense market research may be very simple, but it is essential. It may take less than a day, but don't let the ease with which it can be done mislead you into thinking you can skip or ignore market research. Even the young man who sets out to make money with the family lawn mower sizes up potential market, analyzing its geographical boundaries, his competition, and price ranges. If he formulates his concerns into research questions, he can gather the information quickly and accurately. He can then use it to select sales strategies and predict how much time he must devote to selling, whether he needs to undercut the competition's price to establish a customer base quickly, whether he needs a vehicle to transport his lawn mower, and how much money he can expect to make over the summer.

What Questions Should Research Answer?

Research should provide the information you need to confirm or refute the assumptions you originally made in choosing your business. To begin forming your research questions, go back to the worksheets you did to invent your business. Find the data that convinced you your business was viable.

For the young women who started the tax withholding service for household help, several factors, all untested, made them believe that at least some people (their target market) would find their service valuable. They assume that people who hire baby-sitters want to comply with the withholding laws. They also assume parents will not want to do the paperwork themselves, and they further assume that parents will willingly pay more for baby-sitters (their agents' fee for doing the work plus the employer's share of payroll taxes) to be relieved of the chore.

To formulate their research questions, they simply turn these assumptions into questions: e.g., Will parents hiring baby-sitters be willing to pay an extra fee to be relieved of the task of tax filing? How can they get answers to these questions? The easiest way is to ask—by designing a simple telephone survey. A survey is just an organized way to ask a lot of people for advice (and information).

In a more complex research effort, analysts would first segment their possible market to derive a customer profile or several profiles for customers in different market segments. Fortunately for the two entrepreneurs, their project is simple enough to permit further assumptions regarding their client profile. They begin by making statements like the following, which they know to be true about people who employ baby-sitters.

- Customers will be parents of children too young to be left home alone.

- Some customers will not have access to grandparents or older siblings who can act as baby-sitters.

- Customers will be those from the above populations who go out on a regular basis and must hire outside help to stay with their children.

In administering the questionnaire, the entrepreneurs will introduce themselves, inform the person who answers the phone that they are conducting a survey, and ask the person if he or she is willing to answer a few questions. Upon receiving an affirmative answer, they will ask a qualifying question such as, "Do you ever have an occasion to hire outside baby-sitters to stay with your children?" If the answer is "no," they will thank the person for cooperating and move on to the next call. If the answer is yes, they will proceed with the questionnaire, as follows:

1. How many children would a baby-sitter have to care for at your home? _____

2. What are the ages of the children? _____
   _____

3. Who hires the sitter? Yourself or your husband/wife? _____

4. How frequently do you use sitters? Weekly ____ Monthly ____
   Other ____

5. Do you withhold taxes from their wages or do you expect sitters to be responsible for their own taxes? Employer responsible _____ Sitter responsible _____

NOTE: Few people will admit to a stranger over the phone that they may be in violation of the tax laws. For that reason, the researchers will need to carefully explain the purpose of their survey.

6. If a service were available that would handle the tax filings would you use it? Yes ____ No ____

7. Are you aware that withholding tax will add about 7% to your wage costs? _____

8. In addition to that cost, what is the highest price you would be willing to pay for a service that would relieve you of the responsibility for filing? An additional 10% _____ An additional 15% _____ An additional 20% _____

Evaluating Survey Results

The larger the sample of qualified respondents the young women question, the more accurate the predictive ability of their results. As usual they will resort to common sense to determine when they have sufficient data. This is also a good time to consult a SCORE volunteer or other mentor with marketing experience. In general you can believe the answers to questionnaires, although some respondents will attempt to mislead the interviewer, and others will unconsciously mislead the interviewer in an effort to be agreeable. Pricing information is particularly hard to evaluate for several reasons: (1) people always want the lowest price and may indicate a price in a questionnaire lower than they would actually be willing to pay, and (2) even though they might be willing to pay a higher price, they might also decrease their overall use of baby-sitting services to keep their budget constant.

How many calls should the researchers make to assure a valid sample? Their SCORE consultant advised them to call at least thirty qualified leads (potential clients, or those who answered "yes" to the qualifying question on the questionnaire). Of the thirty, ten indicated they would consider using the service and would be willing to pay an additional fee for doing so. Of those, none indicated that they would pay a 20 percent markup; two indicated they would pay an additional 15 percent, and the remaining eight indicated they would willingly pay only a 10 percent markup. This means that if the two women decide to charge a 15 percent markup, sales in their potential market population would be reduced to 1 in 15; a 10 percent markup would reduce sales to 4 in 15. If they set their price at 15 percent markup, to obtain 100 clients, they will need a sales lead list of 1,500 qualified parents, which they regard as unrealistic. At 10 percent markup, they need only 375 sales leads to reliably yield a client base of 100. (For the sake of simplicity we have omitted their strategy for recruiting baby-sitters, who are also a source of potential clients.)

In addition to the information the young women gather, they must remain alert to external events. The publicity surrounding the baby-sitter tax issue could cause a public outcry that might result in a new law exempting casual baby-sitting services from the requirement. These entrepreneurs, therefore, should budget their development resources to recover their start-up costs quickly.

Potential Market Changes

In addition to measuring the market using the methods described above, you must become sensitive to changes and potential changes in market acceptance. The products and services the market needs and can accept can change rapidly. You need to know that your product or service won't be obsolete by the time you bring it into the market. The advent of wash-and-wear clothing just about eliminated home-based ironing services as a viable source of self-employment. At the same time, trends such as wash-and-wear may also create opportunities, usually highly specialized ones. A few highly skilled home-based ironing services might flourish and even be able to increase fees for service by specializing in expensive and hard-to-care-for fabrics such as Irish linen or silk. Anyone thinking of starting such a service would have to consider these realities.

Market miscalculation is a particularly unpredictable hazard in high-tech industries, and it can catch very sophisticated players. Federal Express's ZapMail service, which sent and delivered faxed documents, was completely destroyed by the fax machine industry, which managed to put faxes in almost every company of any size in a very short time. Now, less than a decade after Federal Express launched, then quickly ended, ZapMail, it seems like a quaint idea given the ubiquitous proliferation of individual fax machines.

The Polaroid Company, the innovative corporation that introduced instant photography, was caught in a similar marketing trap. Polaroid launched instant movie photography, which it called Polavision, at about the same time the camcorder market was ready to explode with affordable home video equipment. Needless to say, instant movie photography's market entry never stood a chance against home video recorders, with their ease of use, low lighting requirements, sound reproduction, and ease of viewing through televisions sets. Both examples involve large, sophisticated companies that should have known better, and it seems clear, applying 20/20 hindsight, that simple research could have predicted the outcome in both cases, but it did not.

Beginning entrepreneurs can also suffer if they misjudge the market. One young inventor developed a lawn mower attachment that held plastic grass-clipping bags in place of the mower's grass catcher. Clippings were deposited directly into the disposal bag, eliminating the need for the grass catcher. When the device was developed, it seemed like a natural product for garden and lawn mower departments in stores; however, by the time the inventor spent several years trying to interest financial backers in his invention, lawn mower manufacturers were coming out with mulching mowers that eliminated the disposal process altogether. The invention was obsolete before it ever reached the market.

Now that the value of market research is clear, let's see how these theories apply to Cindy and the child-care enterprise discussed in the last chapter.

Cindy's Market Research and Test

You will recall that Cindy used gap analysis to develop a value-added, innovative child-care service. She hopes to market her idea to a sufficient number of people to secure ten paying clients twice a week at $15 per child/per visit. She already has several prospect lists and a good general idea about how the business will work. For that reason Cindy decides to conduct her research a little differently from the young women with the tax service. Instead of designing a telephone questionnaire, Cindy designs a brochure describing her service in some detail, which she distributes to her prospect lists. Her research—and market test—will be to follow up on the delivery of the sales brochure with a personal visit or a phone call.

This strategy will give Cindy two advantages: (1) some prospects will accept the service uncritically, giving Cindy some advance sales, and (2) her visits and phone calls will provide valuable direct feedback, which will help with price adjustment, program selection, and other details. What Cindy is doing is more precisely termed market testing rather than research, but for small enterprises there is essentially no difference. *All* marketing is test marketing, and all test marketing is research.

Feedback

Cindy gets a mixed response from her calls, and she is disappointed. Several parents agree to use her service; others hesitate while not saying no directly. Finally, one mother gives Cindy some crucial feedback. Their conversation goes something like this:

Mother: Cindy, you know my husband and I feel absolutely comfortable when you baby-sit for our children, and I'm glad to know you will be available again, but I wonder if you have considered some of the drawbacks to your proposal.

Cindy: Drawbacks? I feel I've planned everything very carefully. What kind of drawbacks do you mean?

Mother: Well, for example, our children are eleven and five. At home their age difference is not really a problem because they each have their own rooms and their own activities, and get along fairly well. But away from home if you put an eleven-year-old in a group of five-year-olds, or a five-year-old in a group of older kids, you may have a rough time.

Cindy: Oh, I see what you mean. As you know, I have handled mixed age groups before. I'm sure I can keep two—or even three—age groups separated and occupied.

Mother: I know you can, Cindy, but you need to make it clear to parents what activities you have planned and exactly what the schedule will be. Another thing you may not have thought about is your fee. Fifteen dollars is very reasonable for baby-sitting, but for people with two children that comes out to $30 for the evening. I know one or two of the parents you baby-sat for have three children, which works out to $45 for the evening. You may lose those clients and some of the families with two children, so you may have to enlarge your prospect list.

By the time she finishes interviewing the parents who received her brochure, Cindy has valuable feedback that allows her to address parents' concerns in her initial sales pitch—her brochure. In addition to the parent concerned about price and age groupings, other parents worried about safety and Cindy's own liabilities. This feedback prompted her to completely childproof her home and add fire extinguishers and smoke detectors. She changed her feeding policy and will provide only food already prepared by take-out restaurants, and she bought a liability insurance policy covering her business. Cindy also took the important step of informing her clients of these revisions to her brochure.

Ongoing Research

Good marketing demands ongoing information in every field, even for the most basic home-based businesses. Common sense marketers must remain aware of changes going on around them. The young women with the tax filing service must remain alert to changes in tax law that would increase or decrease the need for their service. Cindy needs to know about public school programs that might compete with her service. Stay informed about the service you provide, and make an effort to know how your customers feel about how you serve them.

Using Research Data to Develop a Marketing Strategy

Once entrepreneurs have gathered research data, how can they use it to get clients? Marketing strategies, like marketing needs, vary from industry to industry, and from company to company within the same industry. A start-up company and an established corporation in the same business and the same geographic area will develop different marketing plans. Because marketing strategies are so specialized, it is difficult to identify marketing techniques that are equally useful for all types of businesses. Once again, you can extrapolate your own common sense strategies from the following examples.

All viable businesses have some things in common: all have customers or potential customers, market boundaries and quantifiable populations, and a specific message for their potential market that, if properly presented, will produce sales. All customers can be described (profiled); some businesses have more than one customer profile. All market boundaries and populations can be discovered. Therefore, you can determine *what* to say to your market, *whom* to say it to (your customer profile), and *how* to say it (your market medium). Here common sense comes in again because your market research should have provided clues about all of the aforementioned factors.

Taking their baby-sitting tax service one step further, the young women did research that provided them the following information:

Customer profile

Market boundaries and population

Price limitations

Common sense and their SCORE consultant helped them develop a sales strategy, generate leads, and close sales. Because their research indicated that they needed 375 leads to form their client base, their first task is to find those leads. Their telephone questionnaire used a random poll from a confined calling area they had determined to be their market base. However, they knew there had to be a better way to generate leads matching their customer profile than by calling people randomly on the phone. Their first task was to find a list of people who fit the profile. The SCORE consultant suggests that they purchase a list of new parents and parents of small children from a direct marketing firm. These prospects would fit the customer profile. Direct marketers monitor all public records of births, and they track customers of children's boutiques (through credit card data). They sell these lists to anyone who wants them.

The next step is to buy a list, which the women purchase through a list broker. They don't know how to find list brokers, so they find a direct marketing firm in the Yellow Pages and call to ask. The representative of the marketing firm kindly lets them come to the office and go through catalogs of list brokers in the industry until they find what they want. The minimum list purchase is for a thousand names, and most lists cost $40 to $100, with some specialized lists selling for much more. The two women order a list of a thousand names for $40, specifying customer profile and zip codes. They are surprised the list is so inexpensive; the marketing representative explains that the price is low because list brokers "rent" the same names to many customers.

They now have their leads and need to determine how to sell them. They have already rejected newspaper and radio advertising as being too expensive. The SCORE consultant informed them that because they are "niche" marketers, media such as newspapers and radio will not produce an efficient ratio of potential customers to the market area covered. For example, for every hundred people who might see a newspaper ad, only five would be potential customers of the tax-withholding service. On the other hand, a supermarket that advertises in the same newspaper might regard all newspaper readers as potential customers, making the ad an efficient use of the supermarket's marketing budget. The same is true for radio and television advertising, which seeks to blanket rather than target audiences. The SCORE consultant also gave another reason why advertising would not be a wise marketing choice for them: because their service is a new concept, potential customers will need much more information and education about the service than could be practically provided in an advertisement. For this reason new *kinds* of products or services such as personal pagers and mobile phones are rarely introduced to their markets using broad-based advertising.

The women determine that they need some form of direct marketing. Due to the consultant's concern about the need to educate potential clients, they select telemarketing for their sales strategy. They also develop a sales kit consisting of an information sheet explaining how the service works; supplies of W-4 forms for baby-sitters; copies of news articles supporting the need for the service; and several business cards, which they hope will be passed along, generating word-of-mouth sales. Using their questionnaire as the basis for their telephone script, they begin calling prospects on the purchased list. Their initial goal is to get an appointment to drop off the information kit. After the potential customer has a chance to read the materials in the kit, the actual sale is made during a follow-up phone call.

This very labor-intensive sales strategy would not be practical for many businesses, especially those whose products or services are very inexpensive and not likely to generate repeat sales. However, the women's strategy is to establish a client base who will use the service on an ongoing basis and recommend it to other parents. (They have a separate strategy for recruiting baby-sitters.) Therefore, one sale, over time, should produce sufficient revenue to make the extra effort worthwhile.

7

A Case in Entrepreneurship: **WILLIAM S. PALEY**

Major innovation: Pioneered both radio and television broadcasting

William S. Paley's entry into broadcasting was not as a poor, bootstrapping worker at the bottom of the company heap. He started at the top; the trouble was, broadcasting didn't have much of a top when he bought United Independent Broadcasters in 1928 for $500,000.

Paley's introduction to the power of radio came when he experimented with radio advertising for his father's Philadelphia cigar company. He quickly demonstrated that the sales potency of radio advertising was greater than that of print advertising. UIB radio network, owned by friends of Paley's father, was chosen for developing a radio advertising campaign. When the network, which was losing money, came up for sale, Paley convinced his father to let him buy it.

The first thing Paley did was rename the network the Columbia Broadcasting System. He immediately began making fundamental changes that would shape the future of network broadcasting throughout the industry. David Sarnoff was already busily developing his own broadcast empire, NBC radio, through RCA, but Sarnoff's interest was largely in the technology of transmitting programming rather than the commercial relationships between networks and affiliates. Paley shaped that relationship and ultimately determined what listeners would hear coming out of their sets.

He began by renegotiating and clarifying the relationship between the network and its affiliate stations. David McClintock, writing in *Esquire,* explained:

> He devised a much simpler contract, giving the stations attractive incentives but centralizing at the network virtually all

continued

power over the affiliates' broadcasting of network programs. Although the stations' authority was diminished, they liked the Paley plan because it made their own operations much easier. By the beginning of 1929, Paley tripled the number of CBS affiliates. His formula became standard throughout the industry, and though it was modified over the years, the principle of network dominance of local stations became permanent.

Paley formed alliances in Hollywood beginning in 1929, long before broadcasting, through television, would have any opportunity to profit from the movies. However, as he had done with vaudeville entertainers such as Will Rogers by inviting them into radio, he began to find places in broadcasting for entertainers. In *In All His Glory,* the biography of Paley, author Sally Bedell Smith explains Paley's early programming philosophy:

> He prowled the nightclubs and Broadway theaters for performers to put on his network. Although relatively inexperienced, he had good instincts about what made a program work and who could draw a large radio audience. His programming sense may well have originated in his early teens when he had a summer job selling candy at a Chicago theater. Week after week he saw hits and flops, and he could ponder what made the difference. . . . "I am not a highbrow," he once said. "I do not look down on popular taste. Oftentimes popular taste is my taste." . . .

A radio program, he said, "must appeal to either the emotions or the self-interest" of the listener, "not merely to his intellect." Radio broadcasters "cannot calmly broadcast programs we think people ought to listen to if they know what is good for them."

Paley introduced objective and unbiased news reporting to his newscasts by hiring experienced print journalists to produce his news programs. In 1938, at the beginning of World War II in Europe, Paley began live coverage of the war from cities near the front. These broadcasts made Edward R. Murrow a household name. By the end of the war, nearly every home in America had at least one radio, and national television was on the horizon.

In the 1940s he also raided the other networks to make CBS

continued

the top programming network. By 1949 CBS had twelve of the fifteen top shows. At the same time, he changed the relationship of network and advertiser. Previously networks sold air time to ad agencies and programmers responsible for putting the shows together. Paley began selling sponsorship for network-developed programming, which he controlled. That system lasted until well into the television era, when most programming except for news shows was returned to independent production studios and Hollywood movie studios, which produced shows on a contract basis for the networks.

What CBS television took away from the movies in competing for audience, it partially gave back by hiring the Hollywood studios to make TV sitcoms, westerns, and dramas, and the networks eventually began buying made-for-TV movies from the Hollywood studios and independent producers. Another important contribution television made to the movie industry was to purchase the television rights to old Hollywood movies.

Like many entrepreneurs, Paley was not always easy to get along with. He retired as chief executive officer of CBS in 1977, but remained chairman. Then he fired several of his potential successors, finally appointing Thomas Wyman as president in 1980, then chairman in 1983. After Laurance Tisch took over the company, and after a bitter internecine struggle with CBS officials, Tisch reappointed Paley as chairman in 1986. Tisch then sold off CBS divisions and instituted large personnel reductions. Paley by that time was largely powerless in his role as chairman. He died in 1990 at the age of 89.

By the time of his death, Paley, an avid and expert art collector, had assembled an impressive collection, which he left to the Museum of Modern Art in New York and which included paintings by Cezanne, Degas, Gauguin, Matisse, Renoir, and many others. CBS was called the "Tiffany Network," and Paley was called the "father of broadcasting," both for good reasons.

5

PREPARING YOUR BUSINESS PLAN

You will frequently be cautioned about the disastrous consequences of failure to plan. You will rarely be warned about the dangers of overplanning, possibly because most people assume it is impossible to overplan—but that is untrue. At least a few people will be inclined to overplan.

The Dangers of Overplanning

A very talented and creative theater director developed a master plan for a multipurpose nonprofit theater company in a medium-size university town. The plan was complete in every detail; it featured architectural drawings showing exactly how every space in the facility would be used for maximum efficiency. It included daytime uses for school programs and off-season uses for community groups, all of which would generate revenues to help defray the deficit inherent in most live-theater companies. The plan provided pro forma financial statements showing every detail of expenditures and revenue, all backed up with credible research and documentation. Everyone in the community, including the philanthropists who were eager to finance the effort, agreed it was the most brilliant plan for a community project they had ever seen. However, the philanthropists wanted to finance a phased effort over a number of years in order to test the viability of each element. The director countered that the project would work only if launched in its totality as a complete and integrated finished company. He had started the plan in graduate school: building models, researching the market, compiling evidence of the need for live theater in schools and of the economic impact live theater has on the surrounding area. After his refusal to compromise with the philanthropists, he spent the next five years trying to sell the project to other communities before giving up and taking a teaching job. His plan, brilliant as it was, lacked the one element that would have made it viable: a strategy for phasing the project in over a number of years to allow time for fund raising, audience development, and community support (in other words, market development). He invested so much in the plan itself that it became more important than its implementation.

The director was a perfectionist, incapable of finding satisfaction in the compromise resulting from give-and-take transactions, routine events in every phase of entrepreneurship. If you feel you have perfectionist tendencies, practice "good-enough" planning. Don't misunderstand the term; it doesn't mean "less than optimum." It *means* optimum. On the other hand, if doing too much master planning can kill a potential project, doing too little planning can shorten its life expectancy. Less-than-optimum plans omit certain unknown factors that later can result in unwelcome surprises.

The "Good-Enough" Plan

The road map is a "good-enough" representation of the road. It is not improved by adding pictures of the vegetation found along the way. Good-enough is optimum rather than maximum. However, it can't be *less* than optimum. If your plan lacks the figures your banker needs or inaccurately represents your intentions, it isn't good enough. The optimum plan provides all essential information and omits irrelevant details, such as whether the company car is a Chevrolet or Ford. Like common sense research, the good-enough plan saves time, energy, and financial resources you would waste by overelaborating the process just to prove you know all the terms in planning manuals.

Why Prepare a Business Plan?

1. Marketing research provided data to test your assumptions about the viability of your business. That same data along with other information about your business, if presented systematically, will answer questions about how to form, conduct, and expand your business.

2. Developing budgets, describing products and services, and creating customer profiles will eliminate ambiguities about your company's mission and your goals and timetables.

3. A clear and concise business plan will provide the basis for all advertising and promotion copy for future sales programs.

4. If you have partners, a clear business plan will serve as an extension of your partnership agreements and clarify your expectations—from the business and from each other.

5. If you have investors or lenders, or seek them, preparing a good business plan will be the *minimum* they expect from you.

You can begin gathering data for your business plan as soon as the idea for your business solidifies; however, before you can complete the plan, some information will be vital. The information from the last chapter, market research, will allow for sales projections and pricing. You will want to gradually develop other information. Planning is a dynamic process. The business plan can be produced in a marathon of research, number crunching, and brainstorming, but it will benefit if real numbers replace projected numbers as the business progresses. Over a several-year period, close comparison of projected and actual budget figures will help test the accuracy of the assumptions you made when beginning your business. This comparison can also help when you want to use your business plan as a fund-raising tool.

As your business progresses, you may find you need a more elaborate, more detailed business plan. You may have several products or services (profit centers) or you may develop revenue from sources other than your main business. You may take on additional partners, borrow money, hire employees, buy equipment or other capital goods, or encounter external forces such as recession, technological or demographic changes, or other unforeseen events. Your future business plans must reflect these realities; however, at the outset, keep it simple but thorough. If your initial plan becomes too elaborate, your start-up effort might be going in too many directions and a reevaluation might be in order.

Important aspects of the good-enough business plan include the following:

1. It exists

2. It exists on paper

3. It has been evaluated (by you and at least one other person, perhaps a SCORE consultant)

4. It guides your business decisions

5. It reflects reality as closely as possible

Business Plan

Your business plan may consist of the following sections, or at least cover these items:

1. *The name of the enterprise*. Many people starting a business, particularly a one-person free-lance business, neglect to name it, creating a tentative feeling within themselves and others. Some people might view not naming your business as an expression of self-doubt. Give your enterprise a name, even if it's only your own name plus the word "Company." Be sure the address and telephone number appear on all documents. It does no good to create an impressive plan if you make yourself hard to contact.

2. *The legal entity*. After listing the name of your enterprise at the top of your business plan, put the type of ownership in parenthesis; i.e., sole proprietorship, partnership, corporation.

3. *Mission statement*. A mission statement is a definitive statement about what the company does and why it exists. It should be no more than a sentence and can appear on the title page

of the document, underneath the statement about company structure.

4. *Principals or key people.* In an appendix at the end of the plan, list the founders, giving a short background statement and explaining their role in the enterprise.

5. *Introduction* or Executive Summary. This section can appear immediately after the title page and will provide most of the descriptive text for the plan. It should be a short description of the company's main business and might include brief statements of short-, mid-, and long-term goals.

6. *Situation.* Go back to your segmenting exercises in Chapter 3 and summarize the facts or incidents that demonstrated the need your company will fill. Then provide a brief statement about how your company will take advantage of that market opportunity, briefly discussing the market and competition.

7. *Objectives.* Objectives are concrete goals that you can describe numerically and put into a time frame. This section usually outlines the product or service you will introduce and the sales level you want to attain within a given time.

8. *Basic Strategy Statement.* This is a brief calendar of events listing important milestones for accomplishing your objectives.

9. *Product Strategy.* This introduces your sales strategy by placing your product or service within the context of the market need. Your product strategy locates a "position" for your product (and your company) by describing how it fills its niche.

10. *Marketing plan* or sales strategy. Tell how your product or service will be sold. Discuss advertising, if any, direct sales, telemarketing, list development, and other marketing needs. Quantify your marketing plan by listing sales goals.

11. *Financial analysis.* The financial section can consist of several pro forma financial statements plus an operating budget. If your enterprise involves partners, prepare an initial balance

sheet showing any contributed assets, and the resulting obligations, along with any sums already spent or debts incurred.
Each entrepreneur may want to prepare the budget in a slightly
different way, depending on the type of business and any
unique financial needs. Many books are available that detail
methods for meeting almost every individual need.

For example, when Cindy starts the innovative child-care business described earlier, she will need to put a value on the assets her
parents are letting her use, whether she pays for them or not. She
needs to know the value of these assets to evaluate her financial
performance. For example, she should assign a rental value to the
portion of her parent's home she uses on the weekends, calculate
the business portion of the telephone, even estimate the worth of
the small "office" in her bedroom.

Lastly, she needs an operating budget, which is simple. Because
she bills her clients on a monthly basis, her budget is also monthly.
Her only source of income is client billing, so the income side of
her budget consists of one figure: her monthly billing. The expense
side of the budget consists of everything she spends during the
month. If she has expenses that are payable quarterly or annually,
she may want to accrue those on a monthly basis to create a truer
financial picture. For example, Cindy knows she will have to pay
self-employment tax and make estimated-tax deposits quarterly,
so she estimates her total annual tax payment, divides it by twelve,
and puts that amount into her monthly budget expenditures.

Cindy Launches a New Enterprise

Cindy's innovative child-care service differs from day-care centers
and other child-care services in some important respects. First, it
avoids competing with day-care centers by providing its service at
times when most day-care centers are closed. Second, it provides
children with experiences unavailable in most preschools or
schools. Cindy began her enterprise with very rudimentary planning, with simple but realistic start-up budgets, and a pricing strategy that sought to compete with regular baby-sitting services.

Although Cindy's start-up planning was more disorganized than
the good-enough plan recommends, it still covered the essential
elements of her business needs. However, after several years of
successfully running her business, Cindy begins to formulate plans

to enhance her business. It is at this point most entrepreneurs begin seriously looking at developing a full-fledged business plan. Cindy was no different. This time she would need to borrow money (or sell a share of her business to investors). Her plan for her new enterprise is presented as a separate entity from her child-care service.

Because her original segmenting exercises worked so well in her initial business planning, she returns to that method for developing her new venture. Cindy discovers that as her older children became preteenagers and thus too old for child care, she must constantly enlarge her client base just to maintain her level of business, let alone expand. Reading marketing books and talking with her SCORE consultant, Cindy learns that the most fruitful marketing strategies focus on keeping customers already attracted to the business. To do that, Cindy develops a service for a slightly older target customer: her preteen travel camp. The following is the business plan she developed for the second stage of her child-centered business. The format Cindy uses for her "good-enough" business plan can also be easily adapted when the time comes for developing a separate marketing plan.

BUSINESS PLAN

Cindy's Preteen Travel Camp

(Sole Proprietorship: Cindy Smollett, Principal)

210 Alamo Avenue

Anytown, US

Mission: To provide unique and challenging travel and learning experiences that will enhance the maturity and sophistication of our preteen clients.

Introduction

A telephone survey of fifty two-career affluent parents of preteen children revealed some surprising results regarding their access to satisfactory summer activities for their preteen (9–12) children. The survey designer assumed that career-oriented professional couples tend to spend available vacation time traveling with their children. More than 60 percent of respondents indicated that their family vacation tended to be a retreat to a lake, mountain, private ranch, or resort, usually lasting about two weeks and involving the entire family. That left the remainder of the summer with little stimulation for preteens. It was agreed that older preteens were becoming too mature for "little kids" camp, but were too young and immature to travel alone.

Twenty-five percent of respondents indicated they would seriously consider enrolling a child in a one-week travel camp if the program provided activities that were not available close to home.

The Preteen Travel Camp will provide both a travel experience and some unusual nonacademic learning experiences for clients. Each summer will feature travel to different destinations, with travel time about equally divided between one city and one wilderness destination.

The first-year city will be Fort Worth, Texas, where campers will stay in a college dormitory, which will also provide meals. Most of the activities in Fort Worth will focus on visits to its world-famous art museums: the Kimbell, the Amon Carter, and the Modern Art Museum. An art major from one of the local universities will serve as guide and conduct seminars on art history. One half day will be spent at the science museum, including a visit to the planetarium. A university science major will guide that tour. The travelers will also visit the stockyards, now a well-preserved outdoor museum and a historical district. A volunteer from the historical society will serve as a guide. One day will be spent at a nature preserve outside Fort Worth.

continued

At least one meal will be at an ethnic restaurant not found at home and, if possible, travelers will attend a Texas Rangers game.

The group will then fly to Arizona to visit the Grand Canyon for two days. Local package tours will be purchased for the canyon visit. Including travel time the camp will last seven days. One counselor, a photography student, will photograph and videotape portions of the activities. About one week after the completion of the tour, each child will be presented with videotape and a photograph album of the experience.

Long-Term Goals

At the end of the first tour, the program will be evaluated for expansion. Projections indicate the company could comfortably handle as many as ten tours per summer (some running simultaneously) within a five-year period. Some would include overseas travel.

Short-Term and Mid-Term Goals

The first summer would be devoted to developing a prototype tour, developing and testing marketing strategies, and evaluating the service, the costs, and the future potential.

Situation

Market: According to the survey, small cities within the market area lack the cultural amenities found only in large cities: major museums, live theater, sports events, and even the more exotic ethnic restaurants and shops.

Market research focused only on parents of preteen children (one or two were single parents) who could afford the price of the camp. Almost all the interviewees thought the camp was a good idea, and several indicated a willingness to enroll their children. None seemed concerned about the projected price. One expressed interest in enrolling her child in a foreign travel tour.

One parent felt the travel camp would help prepare the children for college, especially for the more prestigious colleges where entering freshmen have diverse life experiences and cultural backgrounds.

continued

Market Area

The initial estimated market area is a cluster of small cities in West Texas that are far from major metropolitan areas. The numerous small towns within the region also will be included in the market strategy.

Competition

The travel camp will have no local competition initially. At present, children who travel do so with parents or other relatives, usually grandparents. Many older teenagers travel in groups or alone, often to foreign countries. Some participate in exchange programs; however, these are nonprofit programs that usually last for a full academic year and involve older teens. Exchange programs would support the business because teens who may later participate in an exchange program will be better prepared if they have had the experience of travel camp.

Objectives

Short term (first summer)

1. Establish one tour of ten participants.

2. Generate revenues of $30,000 for the tour.

3. Realize pre-tax profits of $12,000.

4. Begin to refine marketing techniques to better target market.

Long-term (next five years)

1. Operate ten tours per summer, some concurrently.

2. Generate gross annual revenues of $300,000.

3. Realize pre-tax net profits of $120,000.

4. Begin expansion or spin-off program.

continued

Basic Strategy Statement

1. Complete financing package by October 1, 1994.

2. Complete itinerary and hire on-site counselors by May 1, 1994.

3. Initiate sales-promotion program by November 1, 1994 (close two sales per month beginning January 1995).
   A. Contact all parents previously contacted in market survey.
   B. Provide complete schedule and fee structure.
   C. Schedule first tour for last week of July 1995.
   D. Close sales, collect deposit.
   E. Establish waiting list.

Product Strategy

Market research and conversations with parents of potential clients indicate that parents are now concerned that their children develop cultural sophistication at an early age to compete and function in an increasingly multicultural world. Preteen Travel Camp will position itself to take advantage of this need in several important ways:

1. Provide a travel experience not readily available in any other way

2. Take advantage of cultural resources such as museums, nature preserves, zoos, historic districts

3. Utilize college student counselors who have developed some expertise in their field

continued

Long-Term Development

After expanding the local program to a maximum of ten tours per summer, Cindy's Preteen Travel Camp will establish operations in other areas or will consider franchising the operation to others.

Sales Strategy

A. Products and Services to Be Sold
1. Tours
1 tour/summer 1995
3 tours/summer 1996
5 tours/summer 1997
10 tours/summer 1998
B. Price Structure
1. Tours, per person
$3,000

Primary sales strategy will be through an initial telemarketing to already identified potential clients. This strategy should suffice for the initial tour. In future years several other strategies will be developed and phased in: a peer referral, somewhat similar to that used by children's summer camps, plus direct mail strategies.

Start-Up Budget

Initial preparation, sales material, etc.	$ 2,000
Counselor fees	2,000
On-site counselors	2,000
Plane fares	6,000
Lodging and food	3,000
Insurance	1,000
Working capital	2,000
Total start-up	$18,000

Loan	$10,000
Deferred expenses	8,000
	$18,000

continued

First Summer Tour

Cash Flow

Revenues	Jan	Feb	Mar	Apr	May	Jun	Jul	Total
10 tours @ $3,000*	3,000	3,000	3,000	3,000	3,000		15,000	30,000
Disbursements								
Adv. & sales	400	400	400	400	400			2,000
Salaries							4,000	4,000
Plane fares						6,000		6,000
Lodging & meals							3,000	3,000
Insurance						1,000		1,000
Overhead**	100	100	100	100	100	100	1,400	2,000
Totals	500	500	500	500	500	7,100	8,400	18,000
Profit (loss)								12,000

*Two sales were made each month, and one-half of the fee was collected as a deposit; the remainder was collected just prior to the trip.

**Fee paid to Cindy's child-care service, which provided office space, telephone, copying, faxing, etc.

6

FINANCING YOUR BUSINESS

Most of the enterprises described in this book are examples of "bootstrapping," a term used by *Inc.* magazine and others to refer to self-developing and self-financing enterprises. The "no-investment" approach is not always possible, or even desirable. You may have to raise money, either before you launch your enterprise or shortly thereafter. Nevertheless, most young entrepreneurs don't have access to major sources of funding, such as public stock offerings or bond sales.

One major reason bootstrapping is so desirable for beginning entrepreneurs is that it is often the only viable source of development. Many waste time and energy seeking funding they don't qualify for or have little chance of obtaining. Others fall prey to free-lance investment brokers who take upfront fees for finding investors who never materialize. Venture capital firms are usually a poor source of funding for start-ups. According to Richard M. White, Jr. in *The Entrepreneur's Manual,* few venture capital firms fund start-ups; most are interested in second- and third-round financing, after the enterprise has developed a track record. Venture capital firms also tend to prefer making investments in large dollar amounts, often far greater than the needs of a small enterprise.

To Finance—or Not to Finance

Many small businesses are started at home with no financial help except what the founders provide. Many beginning entrepreneurs eliminate or reduce their need for money by going straight to the source of most start-up support: their own labor. They satisfy their start-up needs in the following ways.

1. *Using Their Own Labor:* You may need to work uncompensated while assembling your business and getting ready for the real, profitable business operations. Regard it as an investment. You may also take in partners who become investors by contributing their own labor.

2. *Starting at Home:* Many businesses can be started at home, requiring no investment in plant or office space.

3. *Using Their Own Equipment:* Do you own a car, a typewriter, computer, calculator, telephone answering machine, mobile phone, or pager? You may already have much of the equipment you will need to start your business.

4. *Taking an Outside Job:* If you are employed, you may elect to keep your job until you save enough to fund your start-up, or you may be able to begin some part of your project while you are employed and able to support it financially.

The question of fund-raising may never arise—or at least not until some major milestone of growth creates a capital need you cannot satisfy through the normal growth in revenues. When that time comes, you will need to be prepared. Those starting a business with complete financial backing usually have a history of starting at least one previous business with little or no outside help.

How can you tell if your business plan will attract financing, or if you should plan a small start-up that's manageable without outside funding?

1. Most venture capital sources automatically eliminate start-ups and concentrate on funding second-stage companies. Your business may be a rare exception; in that event, however, you probably have had some independent evaluation from knowledgeable sources indicating interest. If not, move on to more realistic strategies.

2. Are your financial needs for purchase of inventory or resalable equipment, or for more ephemeral needs such as a marketing effort? Inventory and equipment can serve as collateral for loans; marketing cannot and therefore makes an unattractive risk.

3. What do you personally have at risk? Both lenders and investors want to see your own investment, which they view as evidence of a real commitment.

4. What tangible evidence can you present to investors and lenders that you are a good risk? What evidence have you had that demonstrates your abilities? What is your track record?

Next, assuming you qualify for financing, you need to decide whether you need investors, lenders, or a combination. Both have advantages and disadvantages. The major advantage of borrowing is that you don't surrender any ownership of your company; the major disadvantage is that you will have to pay back the money, usually at a time when the company's resources will be strained even in the most optimistic business scenario. The major advantages and disadvantages of equity sales are just the opposite of borrowing. Equity investment doesn't have to be repaid (although it theoretically can be sold). It becomes part of the capital of the company. The disadvantage is that to get equity you must give up ownership of a substantial part of your business. In both cases you may have to surrender some control, especially if the company experiences subsequent business difficulties.

Finding Funding Sources

Here are some practical funding sources for first-time entrepreneurs.

Partners and Other Principals

This is always the first source to consider. Many investors, including most venture capitalists and all lenders, have rules about how much the enterprise's principals must invest before they're eligible for funding. Principals may sell assets to raise money, or use assets as collateral for bank loans. Such assets may include the following: boats, vacation homes, automobiles, stock portfolios, paid-up insurance, retirement funds, second mortgages on homes (some states do not allow borrowing against home equity except for home improvement), and even portions of ongoing salaries from outside jobs.

Friends and Family

The rules don't change for friends and family members. Collateral and interest rates or equity return should be the same as for banks or venture capitalists.

Banks

Banks are not allowed to make direct investments, but if collateral is sufficient and cash flow projections are adequate to cover repayment, banks are usually happy to deal with new enterprises. Most important, bankers may be a good source for other funding. (A good banker will not give the entrepreneur phone leads, but may give the entrepreneur's name to local investment groups.) Banks may also be a good place to start down the somewhat bureaucratic road to SBA financing.

Investment Clubs

Many professionals with high incomes, such as doctors and lawyers, form investment groups by pooling excess income and searching for investment opportunities, usually locally. Their guidelines are similar to those of venture capitalists (high potential return), but they usually will consider smaller ventures and may be more likely to participate in start-ups than venture capital firms. Investment clubs usually hold informal meetings at breakfast and lunch and give entrepreneurs an opportunity to make a pitch for investment.

SBA Loans

The Small Business Administration has several different programs for lending money to small businesses; the most popular is a program of lending through commercial banks. Qualifying is usually easier than for ordinary commercial loans, and the terms are usually better. And because the government guarantees a portion of SBA loans, bankers also find them a good deal. Drawbacks are the large amount of paperwork to apply (you will probably want to hire a consultant) and the restrictions and reporting requirements for expenditures.

Foundations

Foundations are not normally thought of as a source for investment, but some beginning entrepreneurs may be especially attractive to some foundations. Many foundations make "program-related investments," which means they invest in companies with some connection to their program interests. Foundations may be interested in a specific field such as recycling or in general community improvement, such as providing needed health services to rural communities. They may also invest in a business with the potential to create much-needed jobs in a community. Foundations pay for investments with money from their endowment funds because they are prohibited from using grant money to fund profit-making organizations. To learn more about program-related investment, see Laurie Blum's excellent book, *Free Money for Small Businesses and Entrepreneurs*.

Approaching Funding Sources

Finding funding is similar to what you already did in researching your market and assembling your plan; it is a marketing function. Like your products or services, your fund-raising effort must meet the needs of the potential funders. Therefore, you must understand their needs. Lenders need safety and sufficient collateral. Although they will be gratified to know that the value of your collateral is greater than the loan itself, what they really want is for you to pay back the loan—on time. Investors need an opportunity to make an impressive return on their investment—as much as 25 to 50 percent per year on the original investment. They must also be able to liquidate after a specified amount of time, usually about five years. You need to convince investors there will be a market for their equity after that time. (Their profit will be based on their equity sale, not dividends; they will not expect to earn any dividends from a start-up.)

When you call on potential funders—lenders or investors—structure your presentation as a sales campaign for a major sale (which it is). Even though you have a well-researched business and marketing plan, don't bring anything except your business card when you make your initial approach. Explain that you know they are very busy, but you would like a very brief preliminary meeting to get their advice on preparing your plan. Take notes. Let them do almost all the talking. They will tell you exactly what they seek. Believe them. Ask questions if you feel they haven't covered everything you need to know. You now have valuable data for tailoring the rest of your campaign to meet their desires exactly—even if that entails rewriting your business plan (and perhaps finding partners with strengths you lack). As soon as you get home, send a handwritten thank-you note; then set about preparing and delivering exactly what you agreed on at your meeting.

The Ernst & Young Business Plan Guide also has some good advice for approaching potential funding sources:

1. *Get an introduction if possible.* It is more difficult to interest a reviewer whom you approach cold than one whom you approached via a supportive introduction. Using such an intermediary helps to draw attention to your plan and lends it credibility.

2. *Be selective.* A mass mailing of business plans is usually not a productive course. A more advisable strategy is to approach attractive sources of capital selectively and focus attention on each.

3. *Be prepared to rethink your plan.* If the entrepreneur receives consistently negative responses to your business plan, it may suggest a problem with the plan rather than a consequence of not approaching enough—or the right—sources. In this instance, listen to sources' objections to the plan and reevaluate it.

4. Some sources want to see a summary of a business plan—perhaps the executive summary—rather than the entire plan, in order to facilitate their preliminary evaluation. When a deal has been structured with the anticipated participation of more than

one source, the review can be expedited by having the sources review the plan concurrently.

5. It is not enough to simply identify the appropriate financing organization. The entrepreneur must be careful to identify the appropriate individual within the organization. A large lending organization may have several departments capable of reviewing a business plan. In the same way, a venture capitalist may have specialists in different types or stages of business.*

Beware of Premature Financing

Believe it or not, premature or excessive financing can doom your enterprise as surely as inadequate funding. You can avoid some financing traps by staying away from capital intensive projects. For our purposes, those are projects requiring more money or equipment than entrepreneurial talent. For your first project, choose something labor intensive, that relies on your labor and that of your partners, adding personnel as sales expand. In addition to the operational problems it creates, premature financing may deprive you of control of your enterprise just when it most needs your original, hard-headed vision. Almost all venture capitalists insist on closely monitoring all aspects of development if they invest in your business. This can be a great benefit if your project is a chain of supermarkets or some other enterprise with a rigid developmental methodology. It can be deadly if your enterprise requires the creativity and vision to go against conventional wisdom in developing something unique.

For our purposes any enterprise that cannot expand through revenue growth is capital intensive. This includes banks and insurance underwriters, and many high-tech service industries such as phone companies and TV cable companies because of their intricate and extensive infrastructure (which is part of their capital). Federal Express is a good example of a capital-intensive industry; it could not generate revenues until an extensive delivery network complete with planes and personnel was in place and operating. Many high-tech industries that we think of as capital intensive really aren't, or at least don't have to be. Apple Computer, while

---

*Reprinted by permission of John Wiley & Sons, Inc. from *The Ernst & Young Business Plan Guide* (New York, © 1993), pp. 131–132.

it existed in Steve Jobs's garage, was labor intensive. Many developing technologies are labor intensive in their developmental stages, which is why many computer-related industries developed as Apple did. As late as the middle 1980s, many suppliers of electronic components, especially board assemblies, operated out of small, individually owned and run workshops. As the demand for these components exploded, large investors developed offshore operations in places such as Taiwan and South Korea to supply these components, freeing American entrepreneurs to move on to the next developing technology.

Banks and venture capitalists, acutely aware of financial traps for the unwary entrepreneur, may rescue your enterprise from certain disaster by refusing to make loans or investments. Often, early financing simply compounds later problems by funding your mistakes. Venture capitalists cite these common errors that entrepreneurs finance when they secure funds *before* testing their enterprise through their own homemade efforts.

Poor Prioritization of Expenditures

If cash is available, entrepreneurs may buy equipment they should rent on a short-term basis so they can return equipment that doesn't fulfill their anticipated needs. An auto detail shop may spend $2 per car at the automatic car wash for the first stage of cleaning as opposed to $2,000 to install washing equipment at the shop. That larger investment would be unrecoverable. Some entrepreneurs reason that they save money if they purchase equipment because short-term rentals may seem expensive. However, tying up money in equipment may deprive you of much needed emergency funds later. Other examples of poor prioritization, according to experienced venture capitalists, are hiring personnel before you need them for a specific function and developing future products or services before the current product or service is fully operational.

Poor Control of Financial Resources

Some inexperienced entrepreneurs may be tempted to rent and furnish showy offices or storefronts, which similarly deprive them of more important assets later. They may rationalize these purchases by claiming they are necessary and will impress potential clients. Venture capitalists resent these expenditures because their investment is being squandered, and while potential clients may be reassured by apparent prosperity, if sales are based on facades, greater problems exist that you aren't addressing. Many venture capitalists won't invest in enterprises, no matter how promising, if the entrepreneurs are spending lavish amounts on expensive cars, showy offices, and large expense accounts.

Premature Promotions

Many inexperienced entrepreneurs seriously underestimate the power of advertising. Spending money on premature promotion before you can fulfill the implied promise creates more problems than revenues. One small firm of consultants (who should have known better because they were organization development specialists) ran a back-cover color ad in a trade magazine that backfired. It generated so many inquiries that they spent as much as the ad cost to contact the respondents and refuse their business.

You will know when to take the dreaded step of outside financing. Because the subject is so complex and extensive, you should completely study your needs and research the process before you embark on a fund-raising campaign. Many good books are available that will provide a good starting point for this process. One is particularly useful for entrepreneurs who are moving beyond the beginning stage and becoming serious contenders in their fields: *The Ernst & Young Guide to Raising Capital*. It covers all the usual options for fund raising, plus strategies for evaluating each technique against the particular needs of an enterprise. It describes creative financial sources and strategies that may not occur to anyone not expert in the field of financing.

SETTING UP YOUR
BUSINESS

Organizational chores are unglamourous, time-consuming, and bore many action-oriented entrepreneurs. They are nonetheless essential. A tip for making your organizational life easier: tend to these chores from the very beginning of your business effort. Setting up a bookkeeping system before you make any expenditure or take in any revenue will make your life easier at tax time, when you start scrambling to find receipts and to reconstruct your business transactions. Be faithful to your system: it will keep you out of trouble and support your position in the event of disputes with partners, suppliers, employees, or even the IRS. As you grow, it will provide you essential information about your business performance that's not available from any other source.

A fortunate few entrepreneurs actually enjoy the end-of-the-day and end-of-the-month chores entailed in any enterprise: they are an opportunity to evaluate performance, plan, change strategies, and fine tune. If the company is doing poorly, organizational chores can inspire corrective action; if the company is doing well, evidence of that success can provide a positive, energizing effect.

If you hate record-keeping, decide as soon as you launch your business how you will compensate for that aversion. If you are well-disciplined, you may eventually overcome your distaste for the routine chores entailed in running a business and learn to regard them as the price of self-employment.

Some beginning entrepreneurs who don't enjoy bookkeeping are lucky enough to have a partner or spouse who likes the sense of control and accomplishment of making bookkeeping entries. Others must employ an outside firm as quickly as possible, even at considerable financial sacrifice, to avoid the inevitable chaos that would ensue if they failed to keep their records straight. In addition to a bookkeeping service, these entrepreneurs should also have an accountant prepare taxes and periodically review the way they handle their finances.

Getting Organized

Pay close attention to the following organizational needs.

Legal Status

If you are the only principal, you probably should set up your business as a sole proprietorship. Later, you may investigate the possibility of incorporating. For more than one principal, you need some agreement, usually a partnership agreement, formalizing your relationship. If the enterprise has its own bank account, the bank needs a copy of the partnership agreement or the DBA (Doing Business As) form listing the name of the company if it is different from your own name. In that event, you may also need to file both partnership agreement and DBA forms with your county clerk. The personnel in the clerk's office or the bank officer who opens your account can tell you where to buy these preprinted forms. (Most libraries have books with forms that can be photocopied.) You may want to get some books and research the precise advantages and disadvantages of each type of business formation.

Telephone

Whether you are required to list your telephone as a business or residential phone usually depends on the phone company's interpretation. If you locate your business in a commercial building, you almost certainly will be required to have a business phone; if you remain at home, you may be able to retain your residential listing. The advantage of having a business listing is that you are listed in the Yellow Pages. The disadvantage is that phone rates are higher for business phones.

Business Cards and Stationery

Business cards are an essential selling tool and well worth the ten or fifteen dollar cost for five hundred or one thousand. If one card you hand out is passed on to somebody who becomes a good customer, the cost is more than repaid. Printers and stationery stores that sell business cards have many formats you can select. Having stationery with a letterhead is useful for writing invoices and for correspondence. A tip about addresses: if you are temporarily located at home or in sublet space at another business, consider getting a post office box for your address. It will save reprinting costs if you must move. However, if your business is a store, you will want the physical address on your cards.

Government Regulations

You can call state licensing and tax agencies, usually via a free hotline number, and ask them to send you a packet with information on all permits and licenses you will need. If your business sells products, you probably need a sales tax permit. You may need local permits as well. The Chamber of Commerce may be able to give you all the information you need about local regulations; it will at least be able to tell you whom to call.

Other regulations cover things like compliance with equal opportunity laws, access for the handicapped, and unemployment and worker's compensation insurance. Most of these regulations, except for employee regulations, do not apply to companies with fewer than fifteen employees, so for now they may not be a concern. However, when you enlarge your enterprise or launch a completely new one, it is crucial to comply with all applicable government regulations. Some, such as environmental protection laws, apply regardless of the size of your enterprise. Owners of a new car-detail service may decide against adding oil changes to their services for that reason. Any business providing oil changes must comply with stringent guidelines for disposal of waste oil. Restrictions that limit development of enterprise, particularly complex regulations such as those for waste oil disposal, create a paradox. They drive some entrepreneurs out of business—or into other industries—while creating opportunities for others who enforce the regulations. An entire industry in waste disposal is being developed for that reason. Unfortunately, consumers will pay for these opportunities.

Some regulations apply to specific industries such as banking, broadcasting, and aviation. Beware of entering any highly regulated industry. The regulations always favor the established firms and tend to work to exclude new entrants.

The following list, by no means exhaustive, gives examples of industries that are highly regulated, moderately regulated, and only slightly regulated or unregulated. There has been some shift in the past few years toward deregulation, but the focus has been easing price controls rather than licensing and standards regulation.

Regulation of Industries

Highly Regulated

Medicine

Aviation

Broadcasting

Drug manufacturing

Export/import

Law

Waste management

Oil and gas exploration

Shipping

Agriculture

Fuel manufacturing and retailing

continued

Liquor and cigarette manufacturing and retailing

Banking

Pawn shops

Moderately Regulated

Cosmetology

Food preparation

Construction and contracting

Real estate

Drug and alcohol treatment centers

Counseling

Automobile and other heavy industry

Child-care

Private schools

Insurance

Financial management

Unregulated

Publishing

Advertising and public relations

Entertainment

Building maintenance

Service industries (bookkeeping, landscaping, etc.)

Retailing

Computers

Light manufacturing (clothing, etc.)

Tax Needs

Like your bookkeeping system, it is best to organize your taxes at the very beginning. Generally you will need to be concerned with the following:

Employee Withholdings

If you have employees or if you are set up to pay yourself and your partners a salary, you need a federal tax number. You also need to maintain W-4 forms for all employees, and meticulous payroll records. At the end of the year (January of the following year), you need to issue W-2 forms (or 1099 forms to nonemployee contractors) along with the appropriate reports to the IRS. In the meantime, you need to make tax deposits of withheld taxes periodically according to the size of the liability.

Estimated Taxes

In addition you need to file and pay quarterly taxes based on your expected earnings (nonpayroll) from the business.

The easiest way to accomplish this is to hire an accountant who will guide you through each step and prepare the forms for you. The next easiest way is to call the IRS (800–829–3676). Ask them to send you the necessary forms and booklets (including the form to request a tax number).

Employment Needs

Even if you have only one employee other than yourself, you must become aware of employment regulations, both state and federal. Most regulations regarding hiring practices don't apply until you have a minimum of fifteen employees (Civil Rights Act, Americans with Disabilities Act and others). Some regulations apply to firms with twenty-five employees, and some to those with fifty and more (the Family Leave Act). When you reach one hundred employees, you may be forced to report to many governmental agencies. These regulations are complex and variable, so you should seek specialized help when your work force begins to approach fifteen employees. Meanwhile, you must be aware of minimum-wage requirements and various state "pay-day laws," which stipulate rigid rules for the regularity of employee pay periods. The best place to get help with these needs is your local state employment office, the agency that administers unemployment insurance.

Employee Manuals

It is never too soon to begin formulating policies about vacation, sick leave, work rules, and dress codes. If policies are not written down and given to employees to read, they are hard to enforce. The best way to prepare an employee manual is to review existing manuals. If competitors and colleagues will share this information, take advantage of it; if not, find guidelines at the library.

Bookkeeping

It is strongly recommended that you find a simple computerized bookkeeping system and use it from the very first transaction of your business. Computers are rapidly becoming essential office equipment, much as typewriters and calculators have been for many years. Costs have dropped to the equivalent of a good electric typewriter. You can usually find used equipment much cheaper. Software costs have also declined, and many good accounting packages cost less than $100—some as little as $35—at discount stores. If you are a computer novice, you might want to find a user's club to help you learn how to operate the computer, although manuals for both hardware and software are usually adequate.

The rewards of computerized bookkeeping for even one-person businesses are immense. If maintained accurately and faithfully, they provide meticulous records your accountant will need for preparing your tax returns. Careful records may reduce your accountant's fee because he or she won't have to spend time reconstructing transactions. And as your business grows, the data you accumulate over time will become a valuable asset, particularly if you maintain mailing and customer lists.

8

RUNNING AND GROWING YOUR BUSINESS

Sooner or later you will need to hire employees. That is basic to entrepreneurship. There is no other way you can grow and develop significantly. Finding and managing employees may be the most challenging and most critical function of being an entrepreneur.

Explore Your Management and Organization Growth Needs

This process is similar to the other segmenting exercises. To make sure all your management and organization needs are covered, don't begin with specific job descriptions. Take a blank sheet of paper and head it with two columns: Management Needs and Organization Needs. This method, like the others, is open-ended and spontaneous. Write down needs as they occur to you. You can do this over several days. As you do a task, the particular talent it requires will become apparent. Write it down at that point. Since her business has been examined in earlier chapters, let's take Cindy as an example. Here is her list:

Management Needs	Organizational Needs
Vision of growth	Attention to detail
Awareness of emerging competition	Meticulous record-keeping (diary to document activities in order to report minor bruises, etc., to parents)
Financial management skills	
Planning ability	
Market awareness	Ability to prioritize
Even-tempered and conciliatory	Decision-making skills
Good sales skills	Ability to recover from organization's mistakes
Calm response to agitated parents	(and so on)
(and so on)	

Next, Cindy takes inventory of her own strengths, abilities, and weaknesses. In doing so, she discovers something interesting; her strengths are in filling organizational needs, not management needs.

Using this information she devises her next exercise, which is to invent a process for her first stage of growth. Her SCORE consultant helps her clarify her thinking about hiring by breaking down the process in yet another segmenting exercise. She writes down some requirements for fulfilling staffing needs. They are the following:

1. Knowing whom you need.

2. Knowing how to find them.

3. Knowing how to treat them.

4. Knowing how to reward them.

5. Knowing how to fire them.

Knowing Whom You Need

She next asks herself some clarifying questions about what kind of staff she needs:

1. Do I want to hire someone to *complement* my own abilities (i.e., someone who will compensate for my weaknesses)?

2. Do I want to hire someone to *extend* the work I do (i.e., an assistant or secretary)?

3. Do I want a combination of these two (an alter ego)?

Cindy, being somewhat democratic, decides to find an alter ego, reasoning that her current need is someone who can learn to do everything that needs to be done, even if neither of them can do everything superbly. Like her "good-enough" business plan, this employee will be able to keep the business moving until it is time to take another leap of growth. At her next stage of development—hiring a second person—Cindy will not want an alter ego; she will begin to match employees' talents with specific functions. Cindy's choice is not necessarily right for other entrepreneurs; it may not even be right for Cindy. However, she, like you, must make choices based on common sense, intuition, and rational analysis, all of which can be wrong.

Knowing How to Find Them

Many beginning entrepreneurs find employees the way they find their partners: by hiring their best friends. You may be fortunate enough to have friends whose abilities match the needs of your opening; however, don't count on it. There may be many good reasons for hiring friends; however, there is one very good reason for not doing so: the friendship role will never match the employee role, and conflicts at work may be mistaken for conflicts in your friendship. If you hire a friend, make sure you have a clear agreement to respect the differences between employees and friends.

If Cindy does not hire a friend, how does she find an employee? Two simple ways: she can advertise or recruit.

Employment Ads

This is a passive way to find employees. It is useful for large corporations filling large numbers of routine jobs, such as assembly line workers. Placing an ad in a professional journal is a good way to find highly specialized workers who might be hard to recruit directly. There are also more subtle ways to advertise jobs than through newspaper employment ads. Mentioning the opening to friends and professional colleagues and putting up ads on school and community bulletin boards may get results. Cindy may also advertise through her local state employment agency or commercial employment agencies.

Recruiting

Large companies pay professional recruiters thousands of dollars to find candidates for one job. Recruiting is a proactive way of finding employees and allows more prescreening. You may have observed someone who is already employed whose talents would suit your needs. Recruiting is simply a matter of making contact with that prospect and setting up an interview. Cindy has identified a baby-sitter she already knows, so she chooses to recruit rather than advertise.

Knowing How to Treat Them

There are two major things to consider next: training and supervision.

How to Train Them

Cindy starts her training program with a do-as-I-do approach, supplemented with conversations explaining her methods. Like good-enough planning and common sense research, sometimes the best way to train is the simplest. Obviously if your enterprise is highly technical, this approach may not work, but that itself is common sense.

How to Supervise Them

Supervision can be quantified as well as qualified. Cindy will quantify her supervision by giving her assistant checklists, written directions, and requests for oral reports. This supervision is not just part of training; it will be ongoing. She will *always* be visibly and verbally involved in supervision, even when many tasks become routine. She will clearly express satisfaction for a job well done, and she will *never* overlook lapses. Instead of verbal reprimands, Cindy will retrain, perhaps by saying "Let me show you how I want that done," and then proceed demonstrating without any acrimony.

Knowing How to Reward Them

One of the greatest problems new and small businesses have is employee compensation. Even though Cindy can match the salaries of other small companies, she can't match their employee benefits. She has no retirement plan and no group health insurance. How can she retain good employees? Many small entrepreneurial companies face similar problems, and for many retaining key employees is even more critical than it is for larger companies. Some compensate by giving company shares or stock options in lieu of bonuses or other benefits. That works only if stock options, or stock itself, have some real promise of being valuable one day. Cindy promises her employee a "growth bonus," that is, she will give her first employee a percentage of revenues over and above a certain amount at the end of the year. Even these inducements may not be sufficient to keep employees, and Cindy and other entrepreneurs must be prepared for some employee turnover as a result.

Know How to Fire Them

The best time for Cindy to fire someone is when she hires him or her; in other words, she should establish a probation period. A probation period is a tryout, and the employee is not hired until it's over. If she decides the employee will not work out, she simply declines to hire him or her when the probation ends.

Like other employers, Cindy must avoid arbitrary firings. If she fires someone after the probation period, she should first document her reasons. She needs to make sure the employee is clear about job expectations and aware of infractions prior to termination.

Growing Your Company

Entrepreneurs sometimes have difficulty planning large organizational transitions because the needs of management can change dramatically as the organization grows. During the first stage of Apple Computer's growth, Jobs and Wozniak were the perfect entrepreneurial managers. They found many young people with technical abilities much like their own, people who shared their interest in computers and knew how to expand the market. They inspired hard work and dedication from their staff. Along with their venture capitalists, who provided down-to-earth financial guidance, the management team created a company that quickly ranked among the Fortune 500. Their departure from the company was brutal and acrimonious. The company simply grew beyond what a collegiate entrepreneurial team could handle. Both were bought out and fired. (They founded the company, but they didn't own it. Venture capitalists maintained ultimate control, as is typical.) The lesson for entrepreneurs is clear: When your company needs entrepreneurial management, you must provide it; when it needs institutional management, you must provide it—or you must get out.

Understand Your Company and Its Management Needs

The second need for growing a business is a management style that matches the company's needs. Darryl J. Ellis and Peter P. Pekar, Jr., in *Planning for Nonplanners,* name the types of management needed at three stages of development: "In a young business [or a business in a young industry] the general manager usually should have the characteristics of an entrepreneur, while in a growth business, the manager should be more of a market manager. A mature industry calls for a controller-type administration." They might have added that an entrepreneurial manager is also needed for businesses in declining industries.

Understand Your Industry—Its Opportunities and Limitations

Sometimes the easiest way to grow a business is to start within a growing industry. However, good entrepreneurs know that many opportunities to establish good growth companies exist in mature or declining industries that are ripe for innovation.

If you have gotten this far in your development, the die is already cast; you have selected and formed your company. Your next assignment is to determine where your company fits within the industrial continuum: introductory, growth, mature, or declining. Successful companies exist within each sector, but growth strategies differ depending on where your company fits within the continuum. The strategies offered here can be tailored to help your company survive and grow in the larger economy.

Introductory Stage Industries

Personal computers are no longer an introductory stage industry, although major innovations are continually being introduced. Both hardware and software prices began declining in the mid-1980s and are still declining, indicating a growth industry. However, the innovative introductory phase of the industry is still sufficiently fresh in our memories to serve as a good example. Apple Computer is the prototype of a company formed during an industry's introductory stage. Many companies developing technology for recycling and waste management are likewise innovative/introductory.

Competition to Set Standards

One of the drawbacks of establishing companies in frontier or introductory/innovative industries is that the best ideas and best inventions, or at least those initially perceived as the best, are not always the ones that set the standard when revolutionary technological change is sweeping an industry. Following the wrong standard can doom your business. At the beginning of the automobile age, no one knew for sure that the internal combustion engine would become the standard for powering the automobile. Steam and electric engines were also contenders. Some historians argue that during the early stage of development the steam engine was far superior to the still-developing internal combustion engine, which had major problems with gears and clutches essential for preventing stalling at slow speeds. The steam engine did not require a transmission, making it mechanically simpler, more reliable, and more technologically elegant. Yet, the Stanley brothers, the major manufacturers of steam-engine cars, lacked both the will and the means to expand their products into a wider market. Automotive pioneer Ransom Olds was already in the business of manufacturing internal combustion engines, so it was logical for him to choose the gasoline engine when he began marketing automobiles. Olds and other manufacturers eventually swamped the financially weaker steam-engine industry.

Thomas Edison made the mistake of thinking that direct current, rather than alternating, would set the standard for home wiring. He thus squandered the opportunity to capture the national home electrification market, although, ironically, he made the rise of the electric utility industry possible by demonstrating how to use existing gaslight networks as conduits.

Sony developed the Betamax home video tape format, which was incompatible with its competitors' VHS format. Sony intended to use its market dominance to force Betamax as the industry standard. However, Sony's market strength, great as it was, was not sufficient, and it reluctantly abandoned the Betamax format for the VHS standard.

These stories illustrate two important lessons for the beginning entrepreneur. Regardless of how content you are within your enterprise and how well it satisfies its market, always be aware that innovations are somewhere over the horizon. Sooner or later these innovations will challenge the way your industry or field operates, and you must respond to the challenge, or like the buggy makers, you will go out of business. Second, when presented with an array of innovative choices, don't assume that the one that appears logically superior in the beginning will eventually set the industry standard, as did the gasoline engine. Many factors affect the outcome. Collateral technology can have an impact. In the case of the steam automobile, a system for recycling boiler water was lacking in the early stages of development. Some innovations depend heavily on the strength of infrastructure already in place. Fiber optic technology can transmit cable television, and increase telephone system capacity, but because of the vast coaxial cable network already in place, existing cable companies are fighting phone companies to keep them out of the market. Even fashion trends can affect the acceptability of products. After the election of President Kennedy, who did not wear hats, the men's hat industry virtually disappeared. The intelligent entrepreneur watches developing innovations within the industry closely and then assiduously adapts.

Growth Industries

The personal computer industry entered the growth stage approximately when IBM entered the market and Apple introduced Apple II, during the late 1970s and early 1980s. This was when Michael Dell entered the industry. His role differed from that of Apple's Jobs and Wozniak in one important respect: Jobs and Wozniak were not initially as sales oriented as Dell; they were far more interested in the bells and whistles of the computer and making it do all the (innovative) tricks that would impress their friends in the

Home Brew Club. On the other hand, Dell discovered a major marketing gap: because IBM was accustomed to marketing million dollar mainframe computers and slow to "learn" the PC's vastly different market, it overproduced computers for its dealer network.

Cindy's child-care service is part of a growth industry, although her company is still innovative.

Mature Industries

Most industry falls within the mature category, even though new innovations are constantly needed to keep mature industries from slipping into decline. Mature industries include automobiles, clothing, agriculture and food processing, fast food restaurants, travel and recreation, education, utilities, most retailing, wholesaling, and other manufacturing industries. Mature industries, on the whole, grow at approximately the rate the economy expands. The young man cited earlier who developed a service to transport clients to casinos works within a mature industry—travel and recreation—although his company is innovative.

An entrepreneurial approach to introducing innovation into mature industries is exemplified by The De Beers Company, a very entrepreneurial enterprise despite its age. The company, which is part of a worldwide oligopoly that controls the mining and marketing of diamonds, sought ways in the early part of the century to expand its diamond sales in the United States. It hired a public relations and advertising firm that designed and conducted a marketing campaign that created the "tradition" of the diamond engagement ring. The campaign was so successful that even now the "tradition" is still well ingrained in our cultural psyche. Even without continued promotion, most young women expect to receive a diamond engagement ring from their financés, and most young men still expect to provide it. It is now almost as much a part of our culture as the dowry was in an earlier age. If a random poll were conducted asking people where and when the tradition started, most would guess it was a custom hundreds of years old, possibly with religious significance. (Prior to the De Beers effort, engagement rings were traditionally sapphire.)

As a result of this marketing campaign (and others conducted by De Beers), diamonds maintain a healthy share of the market for luxury goods. Another false notion perpetuated by the oligopoly through public relations is that diamonds have the same scarcity value as gold, and are therefore a hedge against monetary collapse. Their scarcity is strictly controlled by the oligopoly; if breached, the scarcity value of diamonds would collapse. (There are exceptions, such as the Hope Diamond and other famous gems, but the principle remains: diamonds are not the monetary equivalent of gold.)

Declining Industries

An example of a declining industry is typewriters; they are being displaced by computer word processors. Although a market remains for typewriters, they will never regain dominance over word processors. Tobacco is another declining industry, for different reasons. Smoking is becoming less socially acceptable, and so it is increasingly difficult to market tobacco products. It is still possible for entrepreneurs to find opportunities within declining industries. Some specialty publishers have purchased obsolete linotype machines (which have been replaced almost entirely by computer and film) and letterpress presses, which have largely been replaced by litho presses, and are manufacturing lavishly produced limited editions of fine books. As mentioned earlier, the decline of home ironing services has created opportunities for specialized fabric care for linens, silks, and fine cottons.

A Case in Entrepreneurship: **MADAME C. J. WALKER**

Major innovation: Pioneered entry of black women into U.S. business. Provided training and sales opportunities for other black women. First self-made woman millionaire in U.S.

Madame Walker was born Sarah Breedlove shortly after the end of the Civil War and lived until the end of World War I. Her Louisiana sharecropper parents left her an orphan at age seven, victims of yellow fever. A widow at twenty, she moved with her daughter to St. Louis and took a job washing clothes and earned enough to send her daughter to Knoxville College by selling cosmetics to friends.

She moved to Denver in 1905 and took a job cooking for a druggist; there she married C. J. Walker, a newspaper salesman. When her hair started to fall out, she began mixing her own shampoo with antidandruff agents and hair oil, using chemicals supplied by her pharmacist boss. Pleased with the result, she began selling her product door-to-door as the Walker System. The system, which came to her in a dream, involved a hair-straightening method using a combination of shampoo, brushing, and application of hot irons.

At the height of her success, she had a sales force of two thousand black women trained in her own schools as both hairdressers and sales representatives. They operated their own salons using Madame Walker's products.

Madame Walker had a factory in Indianapolis and her own salon in New York City. She lived grandly in a $250,000 mansion at Irvington-on-Hudson, New York, and at her death the Walker Manufacturing Company (now owned by Raymond Randolph of Tuskegee, Alabama) had revenues of $500,000 per year, a substantial sum in 1919. She supported schools, especially the Tuskegee Institute, and charities such as the

continued

NAACP. *Fortune* magazine, in its March 23, 1992, issue, named her to its Business Hall of Fame and concluded its article about her with the following story:

> Attending a convention of the National Negro Business League in 1912, Sarah Breedlove Walker jumped to her feet after the presiding chairman, Booker T. Washington, refused to recognize her. "Surely you are not going to shut the door in my face," she said. "I am a woman who came from the cotton fields of the South. I was promoted from there to the washtub and then to the kitchen. Then I promoted *myself* into the business of manufacturing hair goods, and I built my own factory on my own ground. My object in life is not simply to make money for myself. I use part of what I make in trying to help others."

Washington, dedicated to uplifting blacks through education, may have found this rich, flamboyant woman embarrassing because her fortune and success were based on frivolous cosmetics and hair straightening. However, Caroline Bird, in her book *Enterprising Women,* explains the importance of Walker to her clients, "She dramatized herself to promote her products. Her wealth was an important sales argument for millions of black women whose notions of female beauty were otherwise based on the appearance and lifestyle of whites." A reader's poll in the February 1956 issue of *Ebony* named Madame Walker the first entrant to the Ebony Hall of Fame.

9

CASE HISTORIES

Weed Maintenance Team

Background

The partners are three college students, Jay, Kevin, and Tony. Jay is a senior; Kevin and Tony are sophomores. For the past two summers, the partners had a lucrative painting project. They painted curbside house numbers throughout their town. The first year they covered a quarter of the town, a small city of 100,000. The second year they covered another quarter, and they planned to paint the third quarter this coming summer. However, their enterprise spawned several competing teams, and a drive around the town convinced Jay that the prospect of repeating the success of the past two summers is slim. It is still too soon to repaint the numbers they painted two summers ago, and their competitors have fairly thoroughly covered all the parts of town they missed earlier.

The partners hold a meeting in early May to assess the situation and make plans for the coming summer. Jay took an undergraduate course in economics and understands what has happened with their previous project. He explains to Kevin and Tony, "This is what the professor meant when she said that success spurs competition, but I had thought she was referring only to major industries like computer companies and other growth industries. Who would have thought that something as simple as our business would attract so many imitators?"

"Well, we were making a lot of money after we got our system worked out," says Tony. "When we started we could do only about twenty houses a day; at $5 a house, that's only $33 apiece. We sure didn't attract any competition then. But after we streamlined, with Kevin passing out fliers, me following the next day taking orders and collecting, and Jay running the stencils, we were up to about one hundred houses per day."

"What we were doing," explains Jay, "is called *specialization* in my economics book. Any one of us could do any or all of the jobs—you remember, we all did all the jobs when we first started. But it turned out that when we divided the tasks into three separate jobs, we sped up the process. I know I could work the stencil machine a lot faster when I didn't have to worry about ringing doorbells and collecting money."

Tony says, "Where else can three college students make that kind of money in a summer job, with less than $100 invested in equipment and supplies, without doing any serious work?"

The partner's investment was minimal—even less, Jay points out, than several friends who mowed lawns and had to buy expensive mowers and pickup trucks to haul them around in. Jay had traded his VW Beetle for a pickup truck, then sold it to the partnership for $1,500 at the end of the summer. Stenciling equipment cost less than $100, and the cost of paint and other supplies represented a very small proportion of each sale. At the end of the last summer, they decided to leave $1,000 in the business before distributing the profits. The balance sheet at the beginning of this summer is $1,000 in cash, $1,500 in equipment, and no outstanding debts.

They also agreed to start a "buy-out" fund so that when one partner graduated and moved away, he would be able to "sell" his share of the business back to the partnership. They devised a system so senior partners would accumulate credits, based on earnings and seniority, that would be paid out when they left and replenished at a higher rate by incoming partners. That way the founders would be rewarded for the wealth they were creating by developing the project.

Search for a Competitive Strategy

At first the partners are determined to find some way to beat the competition. They want to continue to enjoy the high-profit quick sale, and easy execution of the house-numbering system they developed. Jay points out that they are not the first companies to face competition. He goes on to describe the competition companies face in the booming computer industry.

"So, what would the computer companies do?" Kevin asks Jay, who seemed to have learned something in his economics class.

"Well, they enlarged the computing capacity of their machines and lowered their prices. The companies that didn't went out of business. In fact, some of the companies that *did* went out of business."

That didn't sound very encouraging to the partners. "How do we enlarge the capacity of our product?" Tony asks. "It's just a house number."

"Well, the right question is: How do we *enhance* our product?" Jay says. "I think the professor would tell us to improve its *utility*."

"How can we do that?" Kevin asks.

"You remember when our first competitors started working? We began adding a white background before painting the numbers. That's an example of an enhanced product."

"That didn't do any good," Tony reminds them. "If you remember, the competitors started copying that the next day."

"That's true," admits Jay, "but maybe we could start using luminous paint." The other partners aren't enthusiastic. The only luminous paint they know about is very expensive and not very sturdy. They doubt it would hold up to the snow, slush, and rain. However, Kevin promises to look into it.

"What about price?" asks Tony. "You said the computer companies lowered their prices at the same time they enhanced their product. Maybe we should lower our price."

However, after a lengthy discussion about price, the partners decide their service (or product) is not price sensitive below the $5 level they charge; that is, lowering the price won't increase their volume enough to make up for revenue lost from the lowered price. Another problem in trying to devise a lower-price strategy is in communicating it to potential customers. Their service is performed on a street-by-street, door-to-door, take-it-or-leave-it basis; customers have no opportunity to comparison shop anyway. Even if they cut their price in half, they reason, it will have little or no impact on anybody's buying decision.

The partners reluctantly decide to search for a new project. They decide to stick as closely as possible to their original, simple guidelines, a project that

Starts at the beginning of summer vacation and ends shortly before school reopens in the fall

Doesn't require expensive equipment or specialized skills

Is easy to market with a very short lead time between making a sales call, closing the sale, and collecting the fee

Is as financially rewarding as the house-number project

Is not susceptible to easy competition

The New Project

They discuss and reject numerous projects. Yard care service is an overcrowded field, and most homeowners are already committed to someone; besides, it is low-paying relative to their old business. Sno-cone concessions at the mall require a larger investment than they are prepared to make, and the work is indoors. Grounds-keeping contracts at larger institutions such as universities and hospitals are annual, so they don't qualify. It seems that nothing is as attractive as their previous project—until Jay excitedly calls for a meeting. "I have our new project," he says.

Jay stopped to visit an elderly aunt and found her on the phone discussing a problem with the city maintenance department. After she hung up the phone, she explained to Jay that the vacant lot next door was owned by someone who lived out of town and could not maintain it. Owners of lots are required to keep grass and weeds mowed to a height not greater than eight inches. If neighbors complain, as Jay's aunt did, city maintenance crews will mow the lot (after notifying the owners and giving them a chance to do it themselves); they bill the owners $75.00. Some lots need to be mowed at least once a month, so costs can mount quickly over the summer.

Given the information Jay has just learned from his aunt, devise a project for the partners, then compare your plan with the one they eventually adopt.

"Seventy-five dollars!" Kevin is surprised. "The going rate for a standard-size lot—with a house on it—is $35, and that includes edging and bagging the clippings."

"The $75 charge must be like a fine," says Jay, "for not maintaining your property. I'll bet people don't like getting those notices to mow, or else."

"I wonder what the notice says," adds Tony.

"I called up the city and asked," says Jay. "They just say that the city has gotten a complaint that the owner is not in compliance with mowing requirements and that if the lot is not mowed within ten days, the city will mow and bill the owner $75."

"So what is the plan?" Tony asks.

Jay outlines his idea about mowing vacant lots, then asks Kevin and Tony to critique it. Here is a brief summary of Jay's plan. If the going rate for mowing yards is $35, it stands to reason that $35 is a reasonable price for vacant lots. Vacant lots can be efficiently mowed using larger tractors with mowing attachments because it isn't necessary to maneuver around buildings and flower beds. With a tractor mower, they could mow a standard-size lot in fifteen minutes and travel to the next job in about fifteen minutes. At that rate they could mow approximately two lots every hour, or between ten and sixteen lots per day. Edging and bagging clippings would be unnecessary because the owner only wants to comply with the maintenance law.

The partners need to conduct a survey to identify all the unmaintained vacant lots in town (or in one section of town). They need to do research to identify and locate the owners. Then they can devise a marketing program to sell the mowing service, and purchase equipment.

How can the partners go about conducting a survey?
How can they easily locate the owners of the property?
Outline a simple plan to market the project.
What are some good ways to purchase mowing equipment?

Kevin is a bit skeptical. "If this is such a good idea, how come all those guys already out mowing lawns aren't doing it?"

"Well," says Jay, somewhat defensive, "where were all the competitors before we began our house-number project?"

"They were waiting for entrepreneurs like us to show them the way, then they jumped right in," says Tony. "What makes you think they won't do the same thing to this project?"

"To answer Kevin's question first, the guys out mowing lawns have tunnel vision. How do they find their clients? They ring doorbells. If the homeowner wants his lawn mowed, they make a deal. When it's finished, they collect their money and leave, maybe getting a commitment to mow again in one or two weeks. There are no doorbells on the vacant lots, so there is no obvious way to make a sale. They are not wrong for ignoring a mowing prospect. They are just doing what works best for them.

"The answer to Tony's question is more complicated. To move in on us in this project, competitors will have to be well organized. By getting heavy-duty equipment and mass marketing our service, we are going for economy of scale. One man with a home lawn mower, or even ten men with ten mowers, will be no competitive threat to us. And even if they got organized and copied our service exactly, there would still be plenty of business to go around because we expect to get repeat business. That was more difficult with painting house numbers because they didn't need to be repainted for at least three years. These lots need to be mowed once a month or more. We will keep a close eye on the competition; if they begin to reduce our business, we'll find ways to outcompete them— improve our service, our marketing techniques, or as a last resort, offer price breaks."

"I guess there is some advantage to working in teams other than companionship," Kevin says, "although I think that is important. It keeps me motivated knowing I have a responsibility to two other people."

"And this economy-of-scale thing," Tony says. "I guess it is important. If I were working alone, I never could—or would—buy a tractor. And I don't think I would know how to devise a marketing plan for this project. Which reminds me, what are we going to do when Jay graduates and depletes our buy-out fund?"

"You will find a new partner," said Jay. "Probably a freshman. There is something else you should consider, and that is hiring an employee rather than taking in a partner. You could hire someone to do any of our jobs and pay them about what they would earn at a fast-food restaurant. Then you can begin to make a profit, which is your reward for the risk of starting a business."

Researching and Planning

As they did with their previous project, the partners divide up the research necessary to devise a workable plan. Physically surveying the town to identify vacant lots is the most time-consuming, so the partners divide this task. They decide to concentrate first on only half the city, so Jay brings out a city map and a red Magic Marker and draws a heavy red line along the street that divides the city. They choose the north side to begin the survey; using the marker, Jay divides the north side into three equal sectors and assigns one sector to each partner. "All we need for this job," he explains, "is a yellow pad and a pencil." He tacks the map onto the bulletin board in the garage workshop at his home, which the partners use for an office.

"And transportation," Kevin adds. He knows Jay will use the partnership pickup truck. Being older, Jay assumes the role of senior partner, and the three of them accept this arrangement. Tony will use his own car, and Kevin, who doesn't have a car, will use his bicycle.

Compiling the addresses of the vacant lots takes about two full days. The partners reassemble then and assign themselves the rest of the planning tasks. Jay volunteers to find out the names and addresses of the owners, Kevin volunteers to devise a marketing plan, and Tony agrees to research mowing equipment.

Jay's Name Research

Jay goes to the public library and talks to a reference librarian. He knows the library has "city directories" that list properties and tenants by address. He doesn't know whether these directories list vacant lots. However, he formed a good habit in school: when faced with a research project, he always explains to the librarian exactly what he intends to do with the information. The tactic pays off this time, as in the past. The librarian explains that the directories will give him some of the information, but are not the best source because directories are updated only yearly, while the same information at the courthouse is updated daily. She advises him to try the office of the county clerk. She also tells him that if he needs phone numbers, he should return to her department with the names and addresses, and she will show him the library's collection of phone books, which cover the entire county.

The desk person at the clerk's office shows Jay how to use the record books to find his information efficiently. She then shows him to a library table where he can spread out his yellow pads and the record books, looking up the owners of the properties. The remainder of Jay's task is easy, but time-consuming. At the end of the third day, he finishes. He counts the names and addresses on his completed list. He has more than 700. Surely that will be enough, he says. Even though they are still unsure of exactly how to use the names and whether they will use mail or telephone sales, they enter the names into a data base on Jay's computer. They can then sort by zip code to discover how many owners live in town and how many live out of town. Sorting also tells them whether one person owns several properties. They also reason that they might be able to sell the data base to a real estate firm, even if they don't use it for mailing.

Kevin's Marketing Plan

While Jay and Tony conduct their searches, Kevin begins to outline a marketing plan. He starts by giving himself some guidelines: the marketing effort must be inexpensive, if possible under a hundred dollars; it must be simple—none of the partners considers himself a good sales person; it must produce immediate, or at least very quick, results. Like the previous one, this is a summer project, and they didn't have months, or even weeks, to build up a client base.

Using Kevin's guidelines, make several suggestions of marketing strategies the partners might investigate.

Kevin checks several marketing books out of the library, but none seem to cover specifically a mowing service for vacant lots. He realizes he will have to tailor the general marketing strategies in the books to a specific plan. He is beginning to feel he needs some combination of direct mail and telemarketing—direct mail for out-of-town owners and telemarketing for those living locally. Long distance telemarketing would be too expensive.

He decides to visit the city maintenance department to see if he can get some help there. Somewhat to his surprise, he finds a very helpful and talkative secretary where he expected to find a bureaucratic runaround. "We don't have any secrets here," she explains. "With the state's new open-records law, any citizen is free to come in and find out anything we happen to be doing."

Kevin discovers that her department sends out about twenty mow-or-else notices per day during the summer. Of those, about half mow before the deadline, and the city mows and bills the other half. The secretary explains that Jay is free to copy the notice list at the end of each day. He then asks if the city ever hires private contractors to do the mowing. Yes, they do, she explains, especially in a wet year such as this when weeds and grass grow fast and city maintenance crews must devote almost full time to mowing parks and roadsides.

She introduces Kevin to the man in charge of issuing contracts, who gives him a stack of forms and tells him to get all his equipment in place and working before he submits a bid. He suggests Kevin call if he has any questions. Kevin has a question right away: If the bid was successful, how many jobs could they expect to get? The man explains that if they proved reliable, they might get as many as twenty per week.

Kevin returns to the office to assess the data he gathered and confer with the partners.

The final marketing strategy has three major elements: (1) a direct mail campaign for owners living outside the local calling area, (2) a telemarketing campaign for all owners living within the local calling area, followed up with mail, and (3) a bid to the city maintenance department for contract work.

Number (3) proves to be the easiest, the fastest, and the first strategy to pay off. The partners agree to mow standard-size lots for the city at a fee of $25 each, contingent on having at least ten lots assigned at one time. The partners know from the previous project how important it is to streamline work. To take one assignment at a time, pick up the work order, drive to the site, mow it, invoice it, and do the paperwork required by the city would be inefficient for one lot. By lowering their unit price from $35 to $25 for the city, they trade the $10 differential for the added efficiency of processing ten orders at one time, a trade-off individual lot owners could not offer them.

The telemarketing campaign is also very simple. They set aside two hours each evening for telephoning (they have only the home numbers of the owners, not their daytime numbers). Because none are really comfortable with telemarketing, they decide to work as a group, although it is inefficient, taking turns on the phone of one-half hour each. They check several books out of the library about telemarketing to get a general idea of how to proceed. All the books recommended writing a telephone "script" to help get the conversation going. They want to avoid calling at meal time, but people eat at different times in the evening; some as early as 6:30 and some as late as 8:30. They also discover after a few calls that some people would rather be interrupted at dinner than during the evening news.

They realize that no matter when they call, some people will be interrupted during something they regard as more important, so they decide to set aside two one-hour periods, 5:30 to 6:30 and 7:30 to 8:30, for telephoning.

They prioritize their list, first calling all those who had received notices from the city. Not surprisingly this list produces a very high acceptance rate, about 50 percent. Faced with paying the city $75 or paying the partners $35 for the same job, almost all the owners are glad to employ the partners, unless they intend to mow themselves or have alternative mowing services available. One or two are suspicious about the close convergence of the notice from the city and the call from the partners, but they still accept the service.

The partners now have enough business to postpone the rest of the telemarketing campaign and mailing until they assess how much repeat business to expect. They are very careful not to overbook and make commitments they can't fulfill.

Tony's Equipment Search

The partners need a small farm tractor and a mowing attachment. How can Tony locate and finance this equipment?

Tony knows the partners don't want to buy a new tractor, but he suspects that farm equipment dealers take trade-ins just as car dealers do, so he searches the classified ad section in the newspaper for tractor ads. His research tells him that the cheapest he could expect to buy a used 45 horsepower, older model tractor is for about $3,000. He also locates several similar tractors listed in equipment auction ads. He knows that dealers who buy equipment at these auctions stop bidding on a $3,000 tractor at about $2,500, so if he attends several auctions and was lucky, he could buy a tractor for just over $2,500. The mowing attachment would cost another $300 or $400.

Because the cash reserve was only $1,000, the partners either have to sell the pickup truck, borrow money from the bank, or both. The partners decide to borrow. Because they already financed the pickup truck and paid it off, they have a track record at the bank, so loan approval is not difficult. They know that is not always the case. If they wanted to borrow money for a mail campaign, office equipment, or other expendable items, they would probably be refused. However, the banker knew the equipment they wanted to buy could be resold for almost as much they would pay for it, and if they used part of their cash reserve for a down payment, the bank's financial risk would be covered.

Banks are interested in more than just covering risk for loans, however. It is important for them to know the partners are reliable and responsible individuals. Although the bank can repossess the equipment and sell it to cover its losses in the event of a loan default, that creates extra work and headaches for bankers, so most bankers want assurance that the loan will be repaid without undue collection efforts on their part.

The outcome of Tony's project is that the partners purchase a 1959, 45 horsepower Ford tractor with a mowing attachment at a farm equipment auction for a total of $3,000. Out of their cash reserve, they budget $150 for additional liability insurance to cover use of the tractor, $250 for transfer tax and state registration (any vehicle driven on public roads must be registered), and $500 for a down payment, leaving $100 in the reserve fund for maintenance and emergencies. The amount of the bank loan is $2,500.

This budget leaves them with nothing to spend on their marketing effort, but the first stage of marketing is their telephone campaign, which costs them only time spent. By the time they will need to initiate their mail campaign, if ever, they will have generated revenues from their initial sales efforts. With their equipment in place, they can also quickly proceed with their contract bid to the city.

Critical Analysis

No matter how well planned or how carefully executed, every new business must solve unanticipated problems, and the partners' business is no exception. Consider the following situations that arise that first summer and advise the partners by selecting one of the responses given or devising your own.

> After the partners complete the telemarketing and city-contract stages of their marketing plan, they still have only enough work to keep their equipment busy about four days per week, whereas they want to work five days per week and, at least during the early summer, sometimes six days per week. They hire a professional mail service to do a direct-mail campaign to the approximately four hundred out-of-town names on their list they did not contact by telephone. The response is disappointing. They receive only fifteen orders which, when checked against the city's notice list, were all found to be owners who received city notice.

Possible Responses

1. The partners decide the best way to get people to respond is to get the city to send notices. They know that the city sends notices when they get a complaint from neighbors. They therefore decide to call in complaints to the city maintenance department, then do a selective mailing to those owners.

2. Using the data from their in-town phone campaign, they determine that a similar campaign, though costly, would be the best way to proceed for out-of-town owners.

3. They suspect the mailing service did not do a good job and decide to do a new mailing, this time using their own ideas and strategies.

> By the middle of the summer, their marketing efforts have snowballed. The city contract manager tells them that one independent contractor has withdrawn and offers them an additional ten jobs per week. They calculate that the additional work could keep an additional mower busy about half-time; however, purchasing an additional tractor and mower would entail stretching out payments beyond the fall, after the mowing season. It would mean finding additional non-mowing work for their equipment.

Possible Responses

1. They decline the additional work, reasoning that their plans are only for a summer project to earn money for school. They are not interested in the additional problems and risks entailed in expansion.

2. They decide to run the equipment in two shifts instead of their present one shift, taking advantage of the long summer daylight hours, and handling extra business without purchasing additional equipment.

3. They decide to purchase the equipment, confident they can hire themselves out to construction contractors after the mowing season, or else sell the additional equipment and recover its cost.

> Jay leaves the partnership at the end of the summer as planned, taking his business buy-out fee from the partners' fund as

agreed. The remaining two partners interview possible replacements. They take this as an opportunity to review the structure of the business to see if they need to make changes.

Possible Responses

1. They select a new partner, telling him his buy-in amount will be equivalent to Jay's buy-out, keeping the amounts balanced. The new partner can spread his buy-in payments over the course of the next work season.

2. Because they are founders, they conclude their share should be greater and inform the new partner that his buy-in amount will be greater than Jay's buy-out.

3. They decide this is a good time to consider hiring someone as an employee rather than as a partner and put off their search until the beginning of the next summer.

Federal Register Alert

Background

Like many unusual businesses, Lisa's Federal Register Alert came about through a combination of fortuitous circumstances. Lisa is preparing to graduate from college with a liberal arts degree. She has no specific career path, and hopes she will find interesting options when company recruiters visit campus to interview graduating seniors. This particular year, however, the number of recruiters has diminished; the few who do come are searching for graduates with technical backgrounds.

Lisa is faced with a more difficult job search than she anticipated, and she is beginning her work life with a heavy debt burden—she got through college, a moderately expensive private institution, on student loans; as soon as she begins work, she will have to begin paying off the loan. Lisa observes that a number of her classmates intend to start their own businesses, either right after graduation or after spending a few years in the corporate world.

Unfortunately, Lisa feels unprepared to become an entrepreneur. She didn't take the "right" courses such as management, finance, or marketing. She has no savings to invest—indeed she has a large loan liability. Family help is not an option. Both her parents work, but they are not in a position of offering financial backing, although she can continue to live at home, at least for now.

If Lisa becomes an entrepreneur, she needs a project that requires little start-up capital, doesn't require sophisticated management skills, and utilizes some skill or expertise she already has.

Formulating Lisa's Project

Lisa became familiar with the Federal Register while researching a paper on endangered species. She spent many hours at the library looking up index references in this massive daily publication, which is the official publication of record for all actions of the federal government. She already knew about the register from two friends of her mother, women who ran a business in Washington that provided research services to college professors seeking federal research grants. She knew that the core of their business was daily searching the Federal Register, then alerting clients to grant possibilities. She knew the business was very profitable, that it was not complex, and didn't require any specialized education.

She also knows the two friends started the business at home with only an idea and several university contacts who became their first clients. Their only investment, other than office supplies, was a subscription to the Federal Register, which then (in the middle 1970s) cost $300 per year. Their largest business expenses in the early days were for photocopying, mailing, and long-distance telephone calls to clients, who were scattered throughout the country. They provided one additional service to their clients: when clients needed to visit granting agencies in Washington, the women smoothed their way by making appointments, local travel arrangements, and providing other small services that made clients' visits pleasant and unharried. Lisa even introduced one of her professors to the service, and he became a client.

Lisa would enjoy doing something similar, but she is reluctant to compete with her mother's friends; besides, they live in Washington, which gives them an edge on providing additional services beyond the research. They recently subscribed to the computerized version of the Federal Register, which is downloaded daily onto their computer and can then be searched more efficiently and quickly. The cost of doing this would be prohibitive for Lisa: $30,000 per year for the computerized service versus $300 for the hard copy. She knew if she started a similar business, she wouldn't even subscribe to the hard copy right away. She would use, at least temporarily, the Federal Register at the library.

Lisa has been thinking more and more about her friends' business after the disppointing job week. While she researches her paper in the Federal Register, she begins a conversation with another young woman she has seen using the register frequently before. Lisa had assumed the young woman was another student.

In fact, she works at a nearby medical center; part of her job is to look up and copy all new regulations or actions pertaining to hospitals. "As you can see," she says, showing Lisa a register entry covering several pages, "some of the articles are filled with extraneous data such as hearing testimony, statistics, and other background information not directly relevant to the action. I also prepare summaries for my bosses; otherwise, they would spend several hours per day reading Federal Register articles."

Lisa is suddenly intrigued. "I would have thought," she says, "that a medical center as large as yours would belong to hospital associations that would do this work for you."

"Well, we do, of course," replies the young woman. "I don't entirely understand why we don't get this stuff predigested from all the lobbying organizations in Washington the hospital belongs to. I think to some extent, we do, but you must remember there are regulations that apply to hospitals besides medical regulations such as collecting for Medicaid and Medicare. We generate a lot of toxic waste, for example, so we have to comply with EPA (Environmental Protection Agency) regulations and lots of personnel and Affirmative Action regulations. Because hospitals like ours can issue bonds for financing, there are yet more nonmedical regulations. It gets more complicated every day. The new Clean Air Act affects us as does the new Americans With Disabilities Act, which just went into effect."

Given what Lisa already knows about her friends' business success researching the Federal Register and this new information, what are some ideas Lisa might explore to start a business?

Lisa explains that she wants to offer a service that would search the Federal Register for clients such as the medical center, and asks if she could meet the administrator. The young woman says, "I bet the hospital would buy your service if it's not too expensive. I'm not the highest paid person at the hospital, but it still costs to send me over here to look up these regulations—and it takes me away from my regular job.''

Lisa calls and makes an appointment with the hospital administrator, although she is still somewhat skeptical that the huge hospital industry doesn't have some central source of instantaneous computer access to information on every new regulation pertaining to hospitals. However, she remembers a conversation with her mother's two friends in Washington about the start of their new business. ''We almost didn't bother to start the business,'' one had said, ''because we assumed that something as obvious as our business would already exist, and probably in an overcrowded field at that. Now, we have plenty of competition, but when we started, no one was offered this service.''

At her meeting with the administrator, Lisa learns that there are many predigested sources of information about regulations and actions in the Federal Register, and the hospital subscribes to many of them, including a number of computer data bases. The hospital also belongs to industry associations in Washington that track legislation and regulation on a moment-by-moment basis. However, the administrator offers several reasons for wanting direct access to the data in the Federal Register. First, there's a time lag in getting information from secondary sources. Sometimes the information is incomplete or comes with an interpretive bias. ''Often, we need the written regulation verbatim,'' he said. Sometimes the interests of the Washington group are at odds with local needs. Direct access also gives a more complete perspective. Finally, a large medical center likes to have some input into the regulation process and having early, direct, and complete access to information on an immediate basis enables it to respond to rules and regulations at the proposal stage or to apply for exceptions. He confirms to Lisa that regulatory compliance is a growing headache for hospitals, taking ever more time, expertise, and expense. He is not satisfied with any of the present efforts to deal with this mounting problem, and one difficulty is simply keeping informed.

What is a reasonable proposal for Lisa to make to the administrator at this point? How can she establish a reasonable fee structure to supply Federal Register information to the hospital without having any precedents to go by?

Lisa offers to supply the information the hospital now obtains by sending an employee to the library to search the Federal Register. She has no idea how to establish a reasonable fee, so she and the administrator agree to compute the time spent by the hospital employee now doing the job, calculate what that time costs the hospital over a year, and pay Lisa a similar amount. She is also free to sell the same information to other clients.

Lisa knows she has the beginnings of a business, but she still isn't quite sure what direction it will or can take, how to expand her client base, or what enhancements she could make to improve her service.

She returns to the library and talks at length with the librarian in charge of government documents. She want to know something about the other users of the Federal Register. The librarian explains that many local government agencies also research articles pertinent to federally mandated programs that apply to their own activities. School districts and even private companies use it. One, a company of geologists and oil developers, came in so often that they eventually got their own subscription. Once, she recalls, the EPA sent out notices to auto salvage businesses instructing them to comply with regulations on the disposal of catalytic converters and freon emission. These businesses certainly could have used a service such as Lisa's, the librarian says. Then they could have called up and ordered the regulation rather than taking time off from work to come to the library. It seems bizarre to both Lisa and the librarian that the EPA didn't simply include a copy of the regulation with the notice.

"I could probably get business from such situations if I advertise my service. I suppose I could put an ad in the Yellow Pages, but if you owned a salvage yard, would you think of looking in the Yellow Pages? And if you did, what heading would you look under?"

"I don't know that Yellow Page advertising would do anything for you in a case such as that. But there is something very simple you could do that would work better," the librarian says. "Leave some business cards on my desk. When people call or come in needing more time than I can give, I will give them your card. When the catalytic converter regulations came out, you probably would have gotten five or ten orders for the same set of regulations. You could afford to charge $10 or $20 for each one, depending on the difficulty of the search, and still be reasonably compensated. You could bill casual users through credit cards and eliminate collection problems."

Lisa appears to be at the point when she can realistically put together a business plan and go to work. Can you devise a feasible business projection for Lisa?

Lisa decides that she will accept casual customers passed on to her by the library, but will concentrate on hospitals. Her mind is teeming with ideas about how to expand her business. The possibilities seem endless. Private industry will soon have to comply with the new disabilities act and will be interested in all reported actions. That alone could keep a researcher busy. However, Lisa knows she needs to stay focused and concentrate on doing a good job for the hospitals. Within the first month she accomplishes the following tasks for her new business.

1. She starts the service for the hospital client and develops a prototype system she thinks will help her expand later. She makes a list, with the help of the administrator, of the kinds of information the hospital will need. Lisa then develops, with the help of the administrator and the librarian, a list of government departments that cover the needs on the list (the Federal Register is indexed by department). When she begins working each day, she sits down with the newly arrived issue of the register and checks the table of contents against her guidelines. If there are relevant entries, she first briefly reviews the contents, then photocopies pertinent entries. (All government publications are copyright-free, so she doesn't need permission to copy or disseminate what she chooses. She is even free to reproduce the document in its entirety and publish it herself.) She then prepares an executive summary of each article and attaches it to the photocopy of the text from the Federal Register. There are five separate documents that first day, so she types up her own table of contents for the batch of documents. One of the articles is a notice of a proposed rule and gives a deadline for submitting public commentary. She knows it is something the administrator will want called to his attention, so she marks it on her table of contents sheet with a highlighter pen. She personally delivers the first day's work to the administrator.

2. She designs a simple corporate identity for her new service. Because her service was somewhat unusual, she decides to make the name of the service as descriptive as possible. She calls it Federal Register Alert. She emblazons the name across the top of her stationery in 36-point type. Underneath the name, in

smaller type, she adds a tag line: Specializing in tracking all Federal Register entries relevant to the hospital industry.

3. She makes six copies of the packet, which she intends to use as sales samples. Next she telephones the administrators of medical centers similar in size and facility to her new client hospital and makes appointments to make a presentation. One administrator tells her he doesn't have time to see her, but invites her to mail her information packet. Another declines to see her, telling her his hospital already subscribes to the Federal Register and will continue doing its own searches. He also invites her to submit her sales packet.

4. Three of the hospitals give Lisa a six-month trial contract for her service; another administrator tells her he will decide at the beginning of the next budget period. The fifth, whom she doesn't meet with personally, tells her his hospital is part of a chain, and all regulatory work is handled directly by the parent company. The sixth, the one with its own Federal Register subscription, refuses to purchase.

5. Lisa begins talking with prospective clients in other industries. Because her town is home to several oil service companies, she concentrates on developing a similar service for the oil industry. She begins to develop a sample kit like the one for the hospitals.

One month after beginning her service, Lisa is serving four hospital clients. Her salary is based on her original fee structure, which was predicated on the estimate of the first hospital administrator whose staff person spent about one-quarter of her time searching the register. Lisa charges all her clients that same amount, so her income is about equivalent to one full-time hospital employee—minus benefits: not a very impressive income for a college graduate.

On the other hand, she tells herself, even though she goes to the library each morning to conduct her search and copy the Federal Register entries, the total time she spends preparing information packets for her clients is probably less than two full days per week. The rest of the time she spends developing and expanding her business. Unfortunately, Lisa doesn't know much about business and doesn't understand that she is becoming an entrepreneur. As a liberal arts major, she is only vaguely aware of what an entrepreneur is, or is supposed to be. However, she is well read, intelligent, and ambitious. She is certainly well aware, especially in the present job market, that she is fortunate to have "stumbled upon" a money-making project she enjoys that is well within her capabilities and appears to offer almost limitless opportunities for expansion. Lisa feels she probably needs some good expert organizational help, but she doesn't know where to get it.

What are several good help sources Lisa might consult at this juncture to develop her business?

Lisa is good at using the library, and decides a good first step is to consult the librarian in government documents, who so far is proving to be a fountain of information and good advice, almost a mentor. While in school, whenever Lisa visited the library, she noticed literature because that was her major. She saw the library as stacks full of novels, perhaps some biography and history, criticism and literary essays. She was dimly aware that somewhere there were also rows of science books, encyclopedias, dictionaries, countless indexes, and other reference works.

Now, the reference librarian introduces her to a whole new world of books touching on every aspect of business: organization, finance, marketing, advertising, merchandising, and entrepreneurship. The librarian helps her select a variety of books. She recommends a basic book on marketing, one on developing entrepreneurial business ventures; and one on entrepreneurship by Peter Drucker that she regards as inspirational. She then gives Lisa the address of a business incubator near the campus, telling Lisa that it might be helpful.

Lisa decides to take a cautious approach. For the first six months she patiently services her hospital clients and develops a wider list of possibilities, including numerous rural and small-town hospitals in the area. She pursues the oil companies, but with much less success. The oil companies are as rigidly regulated as hospitals, but within a much narrower range of regulated activity and they don't answer to accrediting agencies. Many oil companies express greater satisfaction than the hospitals did with the predigested information they receive from their industry associations, both locally and in Washington. The incubator manager suggests that Lisa might offer a service to the associations that represent the oil companies, at least the smaller ones.

She decides to table the oil-industry sales prospect, at least for the time being. She does learn one thing from her research, though. One of the larger independent companies is willing to pay for a custom search to help prepare for an upcoming hearing on whether it can proceed with development of a particular prospect. She feels she is not sufficiently competent yet to undertake anything that complex, so she declines. Because she seems to get a good response from hospitals, she searches for other similar industries to approach. With the help of the librarian, she makes a list that includes residential treatment centers, nursing homes, medical associations, and real estate associations.

Because she prepared her summaries and indexes for the alerts on a computer, she has developed a valuable data base she can search for specific references to Federal Register entries. For that reason, she begins devising a cross-referencing system to locate specific references in the register by searching key words in her own data base.

The incubator manager refers Lisa to a retired executive volunteer who gives her valuable advice, encouragement, and feedback at every step of her development. Because Lisa frequently tells him how much easier it would be to expand her service if she had the Federal Register on her computer disk instead of just the hard copy, he encourages her to find a way to offer the computerized register as part of her business.

Lisa's business plan proposes strategies for enlarging her service enough to justify purchasing one-half share in a subscription to the computerized Federal Register. She locates a regional association of city and county governments that provides economic development services to industry throughout the region. It already subscribes to several on-line data bases that provided information to contractors competing for government contracts and regards Lisa's offer as an opportunity to obtain a valuable data base for half price. Many significant government-contract opportunities are listed in the Federal Register. The assistance the agency gives its clients in bidding for government contracts gives Lisa additional ideas about how she might expand her business in the future.

Critical Analysis

Consider the following situations that arise the first year of the new business and advise Lisa by selecting a response, or devising your own.

Because of the interest in her service, Lisa is convinced she has found a potentially profitable way to build a company; however, despite the help she has gotten from the retired executive volunteer, she finds the business side of her service increasingly chaotic.

Possible Responses

1. Lisa accepts that while she is bright and creative she lacks organization skills, and she looks for a partner who can complement her own strengths.

2. She does not want to give away part of her business to a partner, and she cannot afford to hire help. She asks her retired executive mentor to help her structure a work environment and set up systems within which she can function until she is able to develop a staff.

3. She decides to muddle through her organization problems, trusting that everything will fall into place as the business matures.

> Six months after delivering her first Federal Register Alert to the medical center, Lisa receives a job offer from a newsletter publisher, who tells Lisa that she will be able to develop her publication free of financial constraints by joining his organization. Lisa would be free of organization and financing chores, which she realizes are her weak points, and would receive a good salary; however, she would give up any ownership interest.

Possible Responses

1. Lisa considers the offer to be a sound appraisal of the business she is developing. She does not reject the offer outright, but promises to make a counterproposal in which the publisher would assume a partnership role. At the same time she begins to search for other potential backers.

2. Compared to the disappointing job market she faced at graduation, this offer appears to be more than she ever wanted or expected. She takes it.

3. She decides to remain focused on her own developmental track. She refuses the offer and stifles the temptation to consider it as

an opportunity to seek backing, regarding it as a tempting but dangerous diversion from her goal.

At the end of her first year, Lisa is dismayed to discover that her project has received a lot of attention—and not just from clients and potential clients. Several competing services have surfaced in the area. Some appear to be well financed and well organized. One is a territorial expansion of a company offering similar services in the Northeast.

Possible Responses

1. Lisa ignores the competition, refusing to be distracted from her goals by behaving in what she considers a reactionary way.

2. She collects as much information as possible about the competitors and begins to reassess her service to respond to any predatory incursions by the other firms.

3. She regards the competitors as possible sources of good ideas, possible sources for staff, and possible candidates for merger. She accordingly begins friendly approaches to the competitors.

RESOURCES

Organizations for Students and Educators

American Vocational Association (AVA)
1410 King Street
Alexandria, VA 22314
Phone: (703) 683–3111
FAX: (703) 739–9098

ERIC (Educational Reference and Information Center)
National Institute of Education
Washington, DC 20208
Phone: (202) 254–7934

Junior Achievement
45 E. Clubhouse Drive
Colorado Springs, CO 80906
Phone: (719) 540–8000
FAX: (719) 540–9150

National FFA Organization (NFFAO)
National FFA Center
Box 151605632 Mt. Vernon Memorial Hwy.
Alexandria, VA 22309-0160
Phone: (703) 360–3680
FAX: (703) 360–5524

National Association of Classroom Educators in Business Education
   (NACEBE)
c/o Larry L. Shinn
Lincoln High School
Cambridge City, IN 47327
Phone: (317) 478–3261

Small Business Foundation of America (SBFA)
20 Park Plaza, Ste. 438
Boston, MA 02116
Phone: (617) 350–5096

Association of Collegiate Entrepreneurs (ACE)
1845 North Fairmount
Box 147
Wichita, KS 67208
Phone: (316) 689–3000
   Membership dues: $35.00. (Members are offered discounted
subscriptions to business magazines such as *Inc., Success,* and *En-
trepreneurial Woman.*)

Foundation of Student Communication (FSC)
305 Aaron Burr Hall
Princeton, NJ 08540
Phone: (609) 258–1111

United States Junior COC (USJC)
Formerly: United States Junior Chamber of Commerce; United
   States Jaycees
Box 7
4 W. 21st St.
Tulsa, OK 74121–0007
Phone: (918) 584–2481
FAX: (918) 584–4422

National Trade and Professional Associations

American Business Women's Association (ABWA)
9100 Ward Pkwy.
P.O. Box 8728
Kansas City, MO 64114
Phone: (816) 361–6621
FAX: (816) 361–4991

Asian Business League of San Francisco (ABL-SF)
166 Geary Street, Ste. 405
San Francisco, CA 94108
Phone: (415) 788-4664
FAX: (415) 788-4756

Association of African-American Women Business Owners (BWE)
c/o Brenda Alford
Brasman Research
814 Thayer Avenue, Ste. 202A
Silver Spring, MD 20910
Phone: (301) 565-0258

Center for Entrepreneurial Management, Inc. (CEM)
180 Varick St., Penthouse
New York, NY 10014-4606
Phone: (212) 633-0060
FAX: (212) 627-9247
    Membership fee: $96.00 annually
Because the membership fee includes subscriptions to two magazines (*Inc.* and *Success*) and a newsletter, *The Entrepreneurial Manager,* membership is not as expensive as it first appears.

Center for Family Business (CFB)
5862 Mayfield Road
Box 24268
Cleveland, OH 44124
Phone: (216) 442-0800
FAX: (216) 442-0178

Hispanic Organization of Professionals and Executives (HOPE)
87 Catoctin Court
Silver Spring, MD 20906
Phone: (301) 598-2535

The International Alliance, An Association of Executive and Professional Women (TIA)
8600 LaSalle Road, Ste. 308
Baltimore, MD 21204
Phone: (301) 321-6699
FAX: (301) 823-2410

Latin American Management Association (LAMA)
419 New Jersey Avenue, S.E.
Washington, DC 20003
Phone: (202) 546–3803
FAX: (202) 546–3807

National Association of Private Enterprise (NAPE)
Box 470397
Ft. Worth, TX 76147
Phone: (817) 870–1971, (800) 223–NAPE
FAX: (817) 332–4525

National Association for the Self-Employed (NASE)
2328 Gravel Road
Ft. Worth, TX 76118
Phone: (800) 232–6273
FAX: (817) 595–5456

National Association of Small Business Investment Companies
   (NASBIC)
323 W. 8th Street
5501 Lucas Place
Kansas City, MO 64105
Phone: (816) 374–6708
FAX: (202) 775–9158

National Association of Women Business Owners (NAWBO)
600 S. Federal Street, Ste. 400
Chicago, IL 60605
Phone: (312) 922–0465

National Business Association (NBA)
14875 Landmark Boulevard, Ste. 100
Dallas, TX 75240
Phone: (214) 991–5381, (800) 456–0440
Members are self-employed business people.

National Business League (NBL)
4324 Georgia Avenue N.W.
Washington, DC 20011
Phone: (202) 829–5900
FAX: (202) 726–6141

National Federation of Independent Business (NFIB)
150 W. 20th Avenue
San Mateo, CA 94403
Phone: (415) 341-7441

National Minority Business Council (NMBC)
235 E. 42nd Street
New York, NY 10017
Phone: (212) 573-2385
FAX: (212) 573-7550

National Small Business Benefits Association (NSBBA)
2244 N. Grand Avenue E.
Springfield, IL 62702
Phone: (217) 544-3829
FAX: (217) 544-6585

National Small Business United (NSBU)
1155 15th Street N.W., Ste. 710
Washington, DC 20005
Phone: (202) 293-8830, (800) 345-6728

Young Entrepreneurs Organization (YEO)
1221 Pennsylvania Avenue S.E.
Washington, DC 20003
Phone: (202) 544-7100
FAX: (202) 543-2720

National Business Incubation Association (NBIA)
One President St.
Athens, OH 45701
Phone: (614) 593-4331
FAX: (614) 593-1996

Government Agencies

SCORE/ACE
Service Core of Retired Executives/Active Corps of Executives
Small Business Administration
1441 L Street N.W.
Washington, DC 20416
Phone: (202) 653-6768

Small Business Administration (SBA)
1441 L Street N.W.
Washington, DC 20416
Phone: (202) 653–6832

Minority Business Development Agency (MBDA)
U.S. Department of Commerce
14th Street between Constitution and E streets N.W.
Washington, DC 20230
Phone: (202) 377–1936 or (202) 377–2414

Office of Exporter Credits and Guarantees
Export-Import Bank of the U.S.
811 Vermont Ave. N.W.
Washington, DC 20571
Phone: (800) 424–5201

Office of Innovation Research and Technology
U.S. Small Business Administration
1441 L Street N.W.
Washington, DC 20416
Phone: (202) 653–6458

Office of Small and Disadvantaged Business Utilization (OSDBU)
400 7th Street S.W., Room 9410
Washington, DC 20590
Phone: (202) 366–5335

U.S. Department of Commerce (USDC)
Washington, DC 20230
Phone: (202) 377–3176

For entrepreneurs wanting a comprehensive list of all government programs available to small business, write for the following publications:

Catalog of Federal Domestic Assistance
Office of Management and Budget
Superintendent of Documents
U.S. Government Printing Office
Washington, DC 20402

Small Business Guide to Government
U.S. Small Business Administration
Office of Advocacy
1441 L Street N.W.
Washington, DC 20416

*U.S. Government Books: Publications for Sale by the Government
Printing Office* (Catalog)
For a free copy write:
Catalog
Superintendent of Documents
Stop: MK
Washington, DC 20402
To find information at the city and state level, contact the local chamber of commerce, city planning departments, or your local library.

Suggested Reading List

Alarid, William. *Money Sources for Small Businesses: How You Can Find Private, State, Federal, and Corporate Financing.* Puma, 1991.

Ballas, George, and Dave Hollas. *The Making of an Entrepreneur: Keys to Your Success.* New York: Prentice-Hall, 1980.

Bangs, David H., Jr. *The Start Up Guide: A One-Year Plan for Entrepreneurs.* Portsmouth, NH: Upstart Publications, 1989.

Barber, Hoyt L. *Copyrights, Patents, and Trademarks: Protect Your Rights Worldwide.* Blue Ridge Summit, PA: Liberty House, 1989.

Bennet, Steven J. *Ecopreneuring: The Green Guide to Small Business Opportunities from the Environmental Revolution.* New York: John Wiley & Sons, in press.

Benson, Richard V. *Secrets of Successful Direct Mail.* Lincolnwood: NTC Business Books, 1989.

Bird, Drayton. *Commonsense Direct Marketing,* 3rd ed. Lincolnwood: NTC Business Books, 1994.

Bivins, Thomas. *Handbook for Public Relations Writing,* 2nd ed. Lincolnwood: NTC Business Books, 1991.

Blechman, Bruce, and Jay Conrad. *Guerrilla Financing: Alternative Techniques to Finance Any Small Business.* Boston: Houghton Mifflin, 1991.

Book, Albert C., and C. Dennis Schick. *Fundamentals of Copy & Layout,* 2nd ed. Lincolnwood: NTC Business Books, 1990.

Bond, William J. *Home-Based Mail Order: A Success Guide for Entrepreneurs.* Blue Ridge Summit, PA: Liberty House, 1990.

Breen, George E., and Albert B. Blankenship. *Do-It-Yourself Market Research.* New York: McGraw-Hill, 1989.

Brenner, Gary. *Complete Handbook for the Entrepreneur.* New York: Prentice-Hall, 1989.

Cohen, William A. *The Entrepreneur and Small Business Financial Problem Solver.* New York: John Wiley & Sons, 1989.

Cohn, Mike. *Passing the Torch: Transfer Strategies for Your Family Business.* Blue Ridge Summit, PA: Liberty House, 1989.

Collins, James, and William Lazier. *Beyond Entrepreneurship: Turning Your Business into an Enduring Great Company.* New York: Prentice-Hall, 1992.

Coopers & Lybrand Guide to Growing Your Business (Available from Coopers & Lybrand offices).

Davidson, Jeffrey P. *Marketing to Home-Based Businesses.* Homewood, IL: Business One Irwin, 1991.

Davidson, Robert L. III. *Contracting Your Services.* New York: John Wiley & Sons, 1990.

Donnelly, Robert M. *The Entrepreneur's Planning Guide: Building & Implementing Your Own Business Plan,* rev. ed. New York: Van Nostrand Reinhold, 1991.

Drucker, Peter. *The Practice of Management.* New York: HarperCollins, 1954.

Entrepreneur, editors of. *Entrepreneur Magazine's 111 Businesses You Can Start for Under $10,000.* New York: Bantam Books, 1991.

Foster, Dennis L. *The Encyclopedia of Franchises and Franchising.* New York: Facts on File, 1989.

_____. *The Rating Guide to Franchises* (Revised edition). New York: Facts on File, 1991.

Foster, Ronald M. *The Manager's Guide to Employee Benefits: How to Select and Administer the Best Program for Your Company.* New York: Facts on File.

Friedlander, Mark P., and Gene Gurney. *Handbook of Successful Franchising,* 3rd ed. Blue Ridge Summit, PA: Liberty House, 1989.

Fuller, George. *The Negotiator's Handbook.* New York: Prentice-Hall Press, 1991.

Garner, Daniel R., Robert R. Owne, and Robert P. Conway. *The Ernst &*

Young Guide to Raising Capital. New York: John Wiley & Sons, 1991.

Gaston, Robert. *Finding Private Venture Capital for Your Firm.* New York: John Wiley & Sons, 1989.

Gevirtz, Don L. *The New Entrepreneurs: Innovation in American Business.* New York: Viking Penguin, 1985.

Gilder, George. *Wealth and Poverty.* New York: Basic Books, 1981.

Godfrey, Joline. *Our Wildest Dreams: Women Entrepreneurs Making Money, Having Fun, Doing Good.* New York: HarperCollins, 1992.

Gough, J. W. *The Rise of the Entrepreneur.* New York: Schoken Books, 1969.

Gruenwald, George. *New Product Development: Responding to Market Demands,* 2nd ed. Lincolnwood: NTC Business Books, 1992.

Halloran, James W. *The Entrepreneur's Guide to Starting a Successful Business.* Blue Ridge Summit, PA: Liberty House, TAB Books, 1987.

_____. *The Right Fit: The Entrepreneur's Guide to Finding the Perfect Business.* Blue Ridge Summit, PA: Liberty House, TAB Books, 1988.

Hancock, William A. *The Small Business Legal Advisor.* New York: McGraw-Hill Book Company, 1982.

Hausman, Carl, and Philip Benoit. *Positive Public Relations,* 2nd ed. Blue Ridge Summit, PA: Liberty House, 1989.

Hawken, Paul. *Growing a Business.* New York: Fireside Press, 1987.

Hawkins, Kathleen L., and Peter A. Turia. *Test Your Entrepreneurial I.Q.* New York: Berkley Publishing, 1986.

Hay, Peter. *The Book of Business Anecdotes,* New York: Facts on File, 1990.

Hiebing, Roman G., Jr. *How to Write a Successful Marketing Plan.* Lincolnwood: NTC Business Books, 1991.

_____. *The 1-Day Marketing Plan: Organizing and Completing the Plan That Works.* Lincolnwood: NTC Business Books, 1992.

Holtz, Herman. *Profit from Your Money-Making Ideas: How To Build a New Business or Expand an Existing One.* Charlotte, NC: UMI, 1986.

Hutchinson, Van. *College Cash: How to Earn & Learn as a Student Entrepreneur.* Orlando, FL: Harcourt Brace Jovanovich, 1988.

Ibrahim & Ellis. *Entrepreneurship & Small Business Management: Text, Readings & Cases.* Dubuque, IA: Kendall/Hunt, 1990.

Jacobs, Jane. *The Death and Life of Great American Cities.* New York: Random House, 1961.

————. *The Economy of Cities.* New York: Random House, 1969.

————. *Cities and the Wealth of Nations: Principles of Economic Life.* New York: Random House, 1984.

Jones, Elizabeth F., ed. *You Can Start Your Own Daycare (I Can Books Business Ser.).* Washington, DC: National Association for Education of Young Children, 1990.

Kawaski, Guy. *Selling the Dream: How to Promote Your Product, Company, or Ideas—and Make a Difference—Using Everyday Evangelism.* New York: HarperCollins, 1991.

Keding, Ann, and Thomas H. Bivins. *How to Produce Creative Advertising: Proven Techniques and Computer Applications.* Lincolnwood: NTC Business Books, 1991.

Kern, Coralee Smith, and Tammara Hoffman Wolfgram. *How to Run Your Own Home Business.* Lincolnwood: NTC Business Books, 1989.

Kingsley, Daniel T. *How to Fire an Employee.* New York: Facts on File, 1984.

Kingston, Brett. *Student Entrepreneur's Guide: How to Start and Run Your Own Business.* New York: McGraw Hill, 1990.

Kobs, Jim. *Profitable Direct Marketing.* 2nd ed. Lincolnwood: NTC Business Books, 1992.

Lampe, Thomas R. *Ideas to Marketplace: How to Turn Your Good Ideas into Moneymakers.* Los Angeles: Lowell House, 1991.

Lasser, J. K., Tax Institute. *How to Run a Small Business.* 6th ed. New York: McGraw-Hill, 1989.

Levinson, Jay Conrad. *Guerrilla Marketing Attack.* Boston: Houghton Mifflin, 1989.

————. *Guerrilla Marketing Weapons.* Plume, 1990.

Levitt, Mortimer. *How to Start Your Own Business Without Losing Your Shirt: Secrets of the Artful Entrepreneur.* New York: Atheneum, 1988.

Lieberoff, Allen. *Climb Your Own Ladder: 101 Home Businesses that Can Make You Wealthy.* New York: Fireside Books, 1982.

Lindsay, Crawford. *For Fun & Profit: Self-employment Opportunities in Recreation*. Ancramdale, NY: Live Oak Media, 1984.

Mancuso, Joseph. *The Entrepreneur's Handbook*. Dedham, MA: Artech House, 1974.

Merrill, Ronald L. and Henry D. Sedgwick. *New Venture Handbook: Everything You Need to Know to Start & Run Your Own Business*. New York: AMACOM, 1987.

Nelson, Carl. *Import/Export: How to Profit in International Trade*. Blue Ridge Summit, PA: Liberty House, 1989.

O'Hara, Patrick D. *SBA Loans: A Step-by-Step Guide*. New York: John Wiley & Sons, 1989.

Pendergrast, Thomas F. *E.S.P. (Enterpreneurial Simulation Program)*. Orlando, FL: Harcourt Brace Jovanovich, 1988.

Perry, Robert Laurance. *The 50 Best Low-Investment, High-Profit Franchises*. Englewood Cliffs, NJ: Prentice Hall, 1990.

Ramacitti, David. *Do-It-Yourself Publicity*. New York: AMACOM, 1990.

Reck, Ross. *Turn Your Customers into Your Sales Force*. New York: Prentice-Hall Press, 1991.

Resnik, Paul. *The Small Business Bible: The Make-or-Break Factors for Survival and Success*. New York: John Wiley & Sons, 1988.

Riehm, Sarah L. *The Teenage Entrepreneur's Guide: 50 Money-Making Business Ideas*. Chicago: Surrey Books, 1990.

Ries, Al, and Jack Trout. *Positioning: The Battle for Your Mind*. New York: Warner Books, 1986.

Riolo, Al, and Ellen Greenberg. *The New-Idea Source Book: Starting a Money-Making Business*. Blue Ridge Summit, PA: Liberty House, 1988.

Schultz, Don E. *Sales Promotion Essentials*. Lincolnwood: NTC Business Books.

Siegel, Eric S., Loren A. Schultz, Brian R. Ford, and David C. Carney. *The Ernst & Young Business Plan Guide*. New York: John Wiley & Sons, 1987.

Stevens, Mark. *The Ten-Minute Entrepreneur*. New York: Warner Books, 1985.

Stone, Bob. *Successful Direct Marketing Methods*. 5th ed. Lincolnwood: NTC Business Books, 1994.

Storey, M. John. *Starting Your Own Business: No Money Down.* New York: John Wiley & Sons, 1987.

_____. *Inside America's Fastest Growing Companies.* New York: John Wiley & Sons, 1989.

Timmons, Jeffry A. *New Venture Creation.* Richard D. Irwin, 1985.

_____. *The Entrepreneurial Mind.* New Boston, NH: Brick House, 1989.

Torrence, Ronald. *The Entrepreneurial Survival Handbook.* New York: Prentice-Hall, 1985.

Townsend, Patrick L., with Joan E. Gebhardt. *Commit to Quality.* New York: John Wiley & Sons, 1990.

Tschohl, John. *Achieving Excellence Through Customer Service.* New York: Prentice-Hall Press, 1991.

Turner, Patricia L. *How to Overcome the Fear of Starting Your Own Business.* Redding Ridge, CT: Black Swan Books, 1991.

Varney, Glenn H. *Building Productive Teams: An Action Guide and Resource Book.* San Francisco: Jossey-Bass, 1990.

Vesper, Karl H. *New Venture Strategies.* Englewood Cliffs, NJ: Prentice-Hall, 1980.

Walton, Mary. *Deming Management at Work.* New York: G. P. Putnam's Sons, 1990.

Ward, John. *Creating Effective Boards for Private Enterprise.* San Francisco: Jossey-Bass, 1991.

Weismantel, Guy E., and J. Walter Kisling, Jr. *Managing Growth: Keys to Success for Expanding Companies.* Blue Ridge Summit, PA: Liberty House, 1989.

White, Richard M., Jr. *The Entrepreneur's Manual: Business Start-Ups, Spin-Offs, and Innovative Management.* Radnor, PA: Chilton Book Company, 1977.

Whitehouse, Kay. *Site Selection: Finding and Developing Your Best Location.* Blue Ridge Summit, PA: Liberty House, 1990.

Williams, Trevor I. *The History of Invention: From Stone Axes to Silicon Chips.* New York: Facts on File, 1987.

Wilson, Jerry R. *Word-of-Mouth Marketing.* New York: John Wiley & Sons, 1991.

Winkler, John. *Bargaining for Results*. New York: Facts on File, 1984.

Woy, Patricia A. *Small Businesses that Grow and Grow and Grow*. White Hall, VA: Betterway Publications. 1989.

Yale, David. *The Publicity Handbook: How to Maximize Publicity for Products, Services, and Organizations*. Lincolnwood: NTC Business Books, 1991.

Yate, Martin John. *Hiring the Best*. Bob Adams, 1988.

VGM CAREER BOOKS/CAREERS FOR YOU

OPPORTUNITIES IN
Accounting
Acting
Advertising
Aerospace
Agriculture
Airline
Animal and Pet Care
Architecture
Automotive Service
Banking
Beauty Culture
Biological Sciences
Biotechnology
Book Publishing
Broadcasting
Building Construction Trades
Business Communication
Business Management
Cable Television
CAD/CAM
Carpentry
Chemistry
Child Care
Chiropractic
Civil Engineering
Cleaning Service
Commercial Art and Graphic Design
Computer Maintenance
Computer Science
Counseling & Development
Crafts
Culinary
Customer Service
Data Processing
Dental Care
Desktop Publishing
Direct Marketing
Drafting
Electrical Trades
Electronic and Electrical Engineering
Electronics
Energy
Engineering
Engineering Technology
Environmental
Eye Care
Fashion
Fast Food
Federal Government
Film
Financial
Fire Protection Services
Fitness
Food Services
Foreign Language
Forestry
Government Service
Health and Medical
High Tech
Home Economics
Homecare Services
Hospital Administration
Hotel & Motel Management
Human Resources Management
  Careers
Information Systems
Insurance
Interior Design
International Business
Journalism
Laser Technology
Law
Law Enforcement and Criminal
  Justice
Library and Information Science
Machine Trades
Magazine Publishing

Marine & Maritime
Masonry
Marketing
Materials Science
Mechanical Engineering
Medical Imaging
Medical Technology
Metalworking
Microelectronics
Military
Modeling
Music
Newspaper Publishing
Nonprofit Organizations
Nursing
Nutrition
Occupational Therapy
Office Occupations
Packaging Science
Paralegal Careers
Paramedical Careers
Part-time & Summer Jobs
Performing Arts
Petroleum
Pharmacy
Photography
Physical Therapy
Physician
Plastics
Plumbing & Pipe Fitting
Postal Service
Printing
Property Management
Psychology
Public Health
Public Relations
Purchasing
Real Estate
Recreation and Leisure
Refrigeration and Air Conditioning
Religious Service
Restaurant
Retailing
Robotics
Sales
Secretarial
Securities
Social Science
Social Work
Speech-Language Pathology
Sports & Athletics
Sports Medicine
State and Local Government
Teaching
Technical Communications
Telecommunications
Television and Video
Theatrical Design & Production
Tool and Die
Transportation
Travel
Trucking
Veterinary Medicine
Visual Arts
Vocational and Technical
Warehousing
Waste Management
Welding
Word Processing
Writing
Your Own Service Business

CAREERS IN Accounting; Advertising;
Business; Communications; Computers;
Education; Engineering; Finance;
Health Care; High Tech; Law;
Marketing; Medicine; Science; Social
and Rehabilitation Services

CAREER DIRECTORIES
Careers Encyclopedia
Dictionary of Occupational Titles
Occupational Outlook Handbook

CAREER PLANNING
Admissions Guide to Selective
  Business Schools
Beginning Entrepreneur
Career Planning and Development
  for College Students and Recent
  Graduates
Careers Checklists
Careers for Animal Lovers
Careers for Bookworms
Careers for Computer Buffs
Careers for Crafty People
Careers for Culture Lovers
Careers for Environmental Types
Careers for Film Buffs
Careers for Foreign Language
  Aficionados
Careers for Good Samaritans
Careers for Gourmets
Careers for Nature Lovers
Careers for Numbers Crunchers
Careers for Sport Nuts
Careers for Travel Buffs
Cover Letters They Don't Forget
Guide to Basic Resume Writing
How to Approach an Advertising Agency
  and Walk Away with the Job You Want
How to Bounce Back Quickly After
  Losing Your Job
How to Change Your Career
How to Choose the Right Career
How to Get and Keep
  Your First Job
How to Get into the Right Law School
How to Get People to Do Things
  Your Way
How to Have a Winning Job Interview
How to Jump Start a Stalled Career
How to Land a Better Job
How to Launch Your Career in
  TV News
How to Make the Right Career Moves
How to Market Your College Degree
How to Move from College into a
  Secure Job
How to Negotiate the Raise
  You Deserve
How to Prepare a *Curriculum Vitae*
How to Prepare for College
How to Run Your Own Home Business
How to Succeed in College
How to Succeed in High School
How to Write a Winning Resume
How to Write Your College
  Application Essay
Joyce Lain Kennedy's Career Book
Resumes for Advertising Careers
Resumes for Banking and Financial
  Careers
Resumes for College Students &
  Recent Graduates
Resumes for Communications Careers
Resumes for Education Careers
Resumes for Health and Medical Careers
Resumes for High School Graduates
Resumes for High Tech Careers
Resumes for Midcareer Job Changes
Resumes for Sales and Marketing Careers
Resumes for Scientific and Technical
  Careers
Successful Interviewing for College
  Seniors

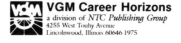

VGM Career Horizons
a division of *NTC Publishing Group*
4255 West Touhy Avenue
Lincolnwood, Illinois 60646-1975